BEHAVIORAL PSYCHOLOGY
(2 Books in 1)

HOW TO ANALYZE PEOPLE
&
ENNEAGRAM

Learn How to Read People's Behaviour, Control Your Emotions and Influence Anyone Understanding Personality Types

By
Richard Campbell

© **Copyright 2019 - All rights reserved.**

The content contained within this book may not be reproduced, duplicated or transmitted without direct written permission from the author or the publisher.

Under no circumstances will any blame or legal responsibility be held against the publisher, or author, for any damages, reparation, or monetary loss due to the information contained within this book. Either directly or indirectly.

Legal Notice:

This book is copyright protected. This book is only for personal use. You cannot amend, distribute, sell, use, quote or paraphrase any part, or the content within this book, without the consent of the author or publisher.

Disclaimer Notice:

Please note the information contained within this document is for educational and entertainment purposes only. All effort has been executed to present accurate, up to date, and reliable, complete information. No warranties of any kind are declared or implied. Readers acknowledge that the author is not engaging in the rendering of legal, financial, medical or professional advice. The content within this book has been derived from various sources. Please consult a licensed professional before attempting any techniques outlined in this book.

By reading this document, the reader agrees that under no circumstances is the author responsible for any losses, direct or indirect, which are incurred as a result of the use of information contained within this document, including, but not limited to, — errors, omissions, or inaccuracies.

How to Analyze People

The Ultimate GUIDE to Mastering the Art of READING PEOPLE through BODY LANGUAGE. Learn TIPS to detect SIGNS of Lying, Attraction, Insecurity, Confidence

Enneagram

The Ultimate Guide to SELF-DISCOVERY through the 9 PERSONALITY TYPES and 27 SUBTYPES – For Beginners Who Wish to Develop their Understanding of Relationships, Leadership, Psychology

Table of Content

How to Analyze People

Introduction 1
Chapter 1 Reading and Interpreting Body Language 4
Chapter 2 Reading the Eyes 11
Chapter 3 Detecting Specific Personality Traits through Body Language .. 22
Chapter 4 Detecting Lies and Deception 28
Chapter 5 Signals of Attraction: How to Know if Someone Likes You 38
Chapter 6 How to Know You are Insecure 46
Chapter 7 How to Influence People 53
Chapter 8 Powerful Tips on How to Read People 58
Chapter 9 Personality Type Explained 72
Chapter 10 The Power of a Handshake 91
Chapter 11 Understand Yourself and Your Behavior: Why Behavior Matters ... 100
Chapter 12 How to Build Rapport Fast 110
Chapter 13 Mistakes to Avoid When Reading Body Language 120
Chapter 14 How to Make a Fantastic First Impression 125
Chapter 15 Dealing With Objections 131
Conclusion 136
References 139

Enneagram

Introduction 147
Chapter 1 The Theory of Enneagram 149
Chapter 2 The Perfectionist 163
Chapter 3 The Helper 173
Chapter 4 The Achiever 183
Chapter 5 The Individualist 194
Chapter 6 The Investigator 205
Chapter 7 The Loyalist 214
Chapter 8 The Enthusiast 222
Chapter 9 The Protector 230
Chapter 10 The Mediator 240
Chapter 11 Testing 250
Conclusion 254
Bibliography 255

HOW TO ANALYZE PEOPLE

Introduction

As long as you live on planet Earth, you will continue to interact with people. From your home to your place of work, to social gatherings, and more, you will meet and associate with other humans. How you survive and thrive well in this ecosystem is a function of how well you know how to relate to people around you. In all forms of communication and interaction, be it in business, romantic, or casual relationships, a good knowledge of how to relate to people effectively matters.

Man is a higher animal, and a complex one at that. Understanding people can be a quite difficult task as a result of the many complexities involved. As if that were not enough, people can be deceptive and mask their true intentions. it takes sound knowledge and an ability to analyze people to see through the veils many people put up.

To make matters worse, the rapid rate at which technology advances has affected human communication. Thanks to social media, which has its advantage of course, many people do not see the need for face to face communication. This has negatively affected our ability to analyze people, as we are only left with drawing conclusions based on messages which could be deceiving.

Knowing how to analyze people will set you apart for success. You get to determine the true and real intention behind every interaction. Also, you get to easily see beyond the mask people put on and know when someone is being sincere or hiding information from you. The art of analyzing people will also help you know if every relationship you find yourself in is worth it, be it business, casual, or romantic, since you will have the skills to determine the true and real intent of your partners.

I, however, understand that many people would like to improve their communication skills as well as learn the art of reading people. As you will find in the pages of this manual, reading people is an essential skill we are all born with. You can, however, sharpen your skills to help you have the upper hand in your interactions with anyone.

Bear in mind that we are not presenting you with a series of some human psychology concepts.

No!

Rather printed on the pages of this manual are tested and proven tips from experts. These are tips that people have been using in their careers, businesses, and other relationship to improve their odds. For instance, some people have to relate with difficult people every day. It could be your boss or a teammate who you cannot avoid. The art of analyzing people will shed light on how to cope with such a situation or person.

Not only will you find actionable steps to improve your relationships with people, but you will also get to learn the skills to keep a smooth relationship. All you need to know about drawing clues from the eyes and body language, detecting dishonesty from all forms of interaction, understanding yourself and your behavior to understand others, avoiding mistakes with reading people and many more skills are imprinted in the pages of this manual. The knowledge you will gain from this book will help you see right through people and know who is being honest based on their body language cues.

Have you ever thought that improving your skill in building rapport will set you apart for success? With anyone you are meeting for the first time, in your business, at the bar, etc., the teachings of this manual can help turn any acquaintance into a friend. You will find here the only two ingredients you need to build a lasting rapport with people, earn their trust, and relate on a fundamental level.

What many people fail to understand about nonverbal communication is that in every interaction, the signals and cues people give with their body are far more important than what they say. This is why you need the right skills to precisely read the subtle nonverbal signals that people are giving. This is critical to your success on every level, be it business, romantic, or casual!

I bet you have never thought that a mere handshake could set the tone for a meeting. In the pages of this manual are practical tips to give the handshake that will pass you off as confident, cheerful, and welcoming.

This is just a brief insight into the wealth of information loaded in this manual. Be assured that by the time you read and apply the teachings of this book, you will develop the skills to have a meaningful relationship, gain the upper hand, and get the best out of every situation.

Have a good read!

Chapter 1
Reading and Interpreting Body Language

The human body is covered with a giant layer of skin. It is with this skin that we make contact with the environment. Not only this, the five senses of the body all have a single, primary purpose - relating with the environment. The environment consists of humans and everything else around us.

Humans live by interaction with each other and the environment. This is basic for survival. For this interaction to be effective, there should be effective communication. Communication between people takes place in many ways. It is not only when you open your mouth and talk to another person that you communicate.

Communication can be verbal, which involves the mouth and ears. However, another aspect of communication that we hardly take note of is nonverbal communication. This makes up a big part of human interaction, but even so, many people lack the skills to decode these signals effectively. Commonly referred to as nonverbal cues or body language, they are subtle, vital signs that convey tons of information, without opening the mouth.

For you to analyze people, it is essential to develop the right skills to decode nonverbal cues. This is crucial for understanding the real intentions of people. Many people might want to fake emotions or hide their true purpose, but nonverbal cues are so powerful, they can help reveal a lot more than a person is saying. I bet you agree that an in-depth knowledge of nonverbal communication and body language can be very helpful in relating with and analyzing people.

It is, however, vital to note that body language reading is not always accurate. This is because it differs for everyone. Aspects like personal habits, cultures, and natural reactions could make this vary from person to person. However, here are some common body language locations and reactions which can help you study and analyze various people over time.

The Eyes

One of the parts of the body that gives detailed information about a person, their feelings, or thoughts are the eyes. This explains why the eyes are referred to as the window to the soul. As a result of this, a whole chapter will be dedicated to exploring the nonverbal cues of the eyes. In communicating with someone, maintaining eye contact is very crucial. It is a natural and essential part of the process. The nature of the eyes during any communication process is so vital that it reveals a lot. The rate at which someone is maintaining eye contact, avoiding gaze, showing a dilated pupil or blinking excessively all have hidden meanings attached to them.

Eye Gaze: Direct eye to eye contact during a conversation means the other party is interested in the conversation and paying attention. Moderation is, however, crucial, as excessive eye contact could be intimidating and downright uncomfortable. Excessive breaking of eye contact signals a distracted person. It could also be that the person is hiding information.

Blinking: While this is a natural process, the frequency of blinking matters a lot. As a rule, when someone is stressed or uncomfortable, blinking tends to be rapid. On the other hand, a person trying to control eye movement could blink infrequently.

Size of the Pupil: You need to be careful when using the pupil size to decode nonverbal communication. Keep in mind that the level of light in the room determines pupil dilation, but there are times that emotions trigger changes in the pupil size. A highly dilated pupil, for instance, can be a pointer to the fact that someone is aroused or interested.

The Mouth

The expression and movement of the mouth is also pretty vital in reading and decoding nonverbal communication. This explains why chewing the bottom lip could signal someone is feeling distressed, fearful, or anxious.

While covering the mouth could be a diplomatic effort of the person while yawning or coughing, it could also be an attempt to keep disapproval hidden. Smiling is also one of the most significant body language signals. However, there are lots of meaning to a smile. It could be genuine or an effort to express sarcasm, false happiness, etc.

Be watchful for the following cues from the mouth and lips when evaluating body signals:

- A heightened or pursed lip could signal distaste or disapproval

- A person might also bite his/her lip when stressed, worried, or anxious

- Someone might cover the mouth to hide emotion, or in a bid to conceal smirks or smiles

Little changes in the mouth can also reveal what another person is feeling. A mouth slightly turned up could indicate someone in a good mood. A mouth slightly turned down, on the other hand, could point to a sad person, or an expression of disapproval.

Gestures

Gestures are one of the simplest, most direct, and apparent body language cues. Some common forms of gestures are pointing and waving, which are used unconsciously and are pretty easy to understand.

It should be pointed out, however, that some gestures could be cultural. Hence, a gesture might have a different meaning, depending on the location. Here are common gestures alongside the meaning they convey:

- In some culture or circumstance, a clenched fist is an indication of anger, while it means solidarity in other cultures.

- Thumbs up and thumbs down respectively are used as gestures to indicate approval and disapproval. They're pretty common in social media

- When you make the V sign, done by lifting the middle finger and the index and keeping them apart to form the V shape, it signals victory or peace in some cultures. People from Australia or the United Kingdom might find this offensive, especially when you have your back hand facing outward.

The Arms and Legs

Every part of the body has some role to play in conveying nonverbal communication signals. Crossed arms, for instance, are a clear indication of being defensive. Likewise, a person who crosses their legs might signal dislike or discomfort towards another person.

Other subtle cues from the arms and legs include an extension of the arms widely in an attempt to appear commanding. On the other hand, trying to minimize body size is an attempt to get away from the spotlight. Other cues that might help you evaluate body signals are:

- Crossed arms indicate a person feeling closed off or self-protective.

- A pose with the arms akimbo is a position of power, indicating someone ready to take control. This is why many superheroes are depicted in this pose.
- Excessive fidgeting or tapping the fingers is a sign of being boredom, frustration, or impatience.

Posture

The manner in which we carry ourselves has an equally significant role to play in expressing body language. Posture is said to be how we hold our body. It can reveal a ton of information about someone as well as their characteristics, for instance, whether the person is submissive, open or confident, etc.

A good example is sitting up straight, which indicates interest in the conversation. This is in contrast to slouching, which shows indifference or boredom. The body's posture is also a very vital part of body language. Take note of the following:

- A friendly, open, and welcoming posture will have the body trunk open and exposed.
- Unfriendly posture, which can sometimes indicate anxiety, will involve hiding the body trunk. This posture is characterized by keeping the arms and legs crossed.

Head Movements

Just like the eyes, head movement is an important aspect of body language that reveals tons of information. Anyone who is, however, ignorant of this body language will have no clue whatsoever what head movement signifies.

Picture a salesperson trying to close a deal with a potential client. As he proceeds with his sales pitch, the prospect nods hurriedly and the salesman keeps blabbing on and on about what he is offering. This salesman is obviously clueless to the fact that the candidate is not interested in his contract.

Here is another instance of a salesman trying to close a deal. As he goes about his sales pitch, the prospect slightly tilts their head backward. The salesman, ignorant of this body cue, makes no effort to shed more light on what confused his prospect. He is obviously unaware of the suspicion evident in the prospect's body language.

In interpreting head movement, take note of the following:

- When a person loses interest in a conversation, they offer quick and successive nods. The salesman in our first example, trying to convince an uninterested buyer, would have saved himself time and effort.
- A person interested in a discussion will offer a slow nod, or slightly tilt their head. A person trying to close a deal or make a sale should watch out for these body cues.
- When a person tilts their head backward during the conversation, it signals suspicion or uncertainty. This is a cue to clarify yourself or shed more light on the point that triggered this reaction. The salesman in our last example could have used this to shed more light on his previous point, rather than blabbing on and on.
- A person scratching their neck or jaw may disagree with whatever issue is being discussed. Take this as a cue to ask for the person's opinion on the matter at hand.
- When in a gathering or at a meeting and you are not sure who calls the shots, all you have to do is find out who the majority of the people are looking at. The decision maker gets more attention.

Chapter 2
Reading the Eyes

One of the keys to effectively reading and analyzing people is to approach them with an open mind. In other words, not everyone is against you, out to get you, or has an ulterior motive. People go about their daily activities with various ranges of emotions that can be linked to their eyes. The eyes hold a cue that can give a glimpse into what is going on in their mind. While the eyes might not really reveal someone's entire personality, they help you understand the state of mind of the person at that moment. Even kids and little ones can get an idea of someone's thoughts just by looking at their eyes and responding appropriately.

This chapter will detail how to read people by examining eye movement and what these movements mean. A lot of nonverbal cues can be communicated via the eyes; hence, we are dedicating a whole chapter to it. Part of the reason some people consider dark glasses is to prevent people from reading their eyes. Consider gangsters and others attempting to appear powerful - they use dark glasses to hide their emotions.

Eye behavior interpretation starts at a young age. Even infants as young as seven months old can respond to various eye gazes. By nature, babies can decipher the different types of eye cues that reveal bonding. This helps hone their ability to unconsciously develop social cues that lay the foundation for their social skills.

Eye Cues from Eye Movement

Looking Up

People often look up when they are thinking. This is because someone is trying to construct mental pictures in their head or is thinking critically. A person in a debate or making a speech could, in a bid to recall their points, also look up.

When someone is trying to recall a memory, they will look up and to the left. When someone is trying to make a mental picture, they will often look up and to the right (this often betrays a liar). You, however, need to be careful with this, as it could be reversed. If you want to be sure, establish a baseline by asking the person to recall a simple fact. More on this on the chapter that sheds light on the mistakes people make when reading people.

When people are bored, they also look up. This might indicate someone seeking something interesting in the environment.

Looking Down

Looking down removes direct eye to eye contact with the other person. It could be a sign of submission, or when you are trying to show deference to someone. This is not surprising, as the way you look at someone could convey power and submission.

Aside from conveying submission, looking down could be an indication of someone feeling guilty.

A person who looks down and to the left could be talking to themselves. See if there is a slight movement of the lips. On the other hand, looking down towards the right could be an indication of a person taking care of their inner emotions.

It is important, however, to note that there are cultures where eye contact is seen as rude. People might look down in such cases to communicate respect.

Looking Sideways

The field of vision of a person is in the horizontal plane. Hence, a person looking sideways could be distracted from what is before them.

When someone quickly glances sideways, the person could be checking out the distraction to ascertain if it is an interest or a threat. It could also be used to express displeasure.

Lateral Movement

Eyes moving from side to side could point to lying, which could be expressed as the person considering an escape route should they be caught.

Someone looking towards the door could reveal boredom, especially when in a meeting, as the door signals an escape from the current situation. A conspiratorial person could also look sideways as if they are checking if anyone is following their speech.

Other Cues from the Eyes

Some other nonverbal clues that could be detected from the eyes are:

Eye-Blocking

Shielding or covering the eyes is common when people are repelled by what they see. This does not only relate to sight - when people hear what is not pleasant, you will also see them covering their eyes, which often is an expression of an uncomfortable situation.

Eye-blocking could also be expressed through rubbing of the eyes or excessive blinking. Someone could also block the eyes as a display of consternation or disagreement. This is a habit that was built into us by nature.

Pupil Size

The size of our pupils also indicates some emotions. When we are in low light or see something stimulating, the pupils dilate. If we love our surroundings, the pupils dilate in a bid to take in more of the surroundings. This is why people in a romantic relationship can often be seen with their pupils dilated.

Advertisers that use female models widen the pupils in their ads. All of this is to make their product appealing to would-be customers.

On the other hand, the pupils constrict and block out an offensive image when we see something that is not pleasing.

Squinting

Just like eye blocking above, people squint at you when they are not pleased with the conversation. This is often in an attempt to block out what irritates them. Hence, while making a presentation or having a discussion and you notice anyone squint, it is good to take a pause and use that as a clue to clarify your last point.

Eyebrows

The eyebrows often draw attention and send subtle nonverbal communication signals. Someone could use their eyebrows when making a compelling point in an attempt to emphasize their point. It is also an indication of peace, an expression of interest in communication, and a desire to communicate better.

Eyes and Romantic Relationship

Eye movement is pretty significant in courtship. In a romantic relationship, here are some ways in which we use or eyes:

- Ladies, in a bid to look defenseless and helpless, will raise their eyebrows up to the forehead. This triggers the release of hormones in a man to defend the lady.
- Gazing at another person stimulates them in a bid to return an attraction.
- There is a solid move for a woman who wants to flirt. This takes place in the form of a sideways glance over a raised shoulder. This expresses the curve and

smoothness of a woman's face, exposing the vulnerability of the neck.

Gazing

When you look at something or someone, you are likely interested in the person or thing. Besides, in looking at something, other people that look in the direction of your eyes will be compelled to follow your gaze to access what has gotten your interest.

When gazing at someone, it is usually at the eye level or above, or one could be looking at someone in general without a particular focus on the person or immediate environment.

When you lock gazes with someone, and the person returns the gaze at eye level, it could be love. If the eyes access the lower part of your body, it could be lust. You, however, need to discover the part of the body where the eyes are fixed. Looking at the lips might indicate a desire to kiss. Looking at the breast or other sexual regions could indicate the intention of a sexual relationship.

Looking at a whole person up and down means you are sizing them up. It could be either as a sexual partner or a potential threat. Where the gaze lingers often reveals the true intention. It could be pretty insulting, as it shows the position of dominance because the other person is communicating authority: "I am your superior, your opinions do not matter, and you will submit to me."

Looking at another person's forehead could indicate a distracted person. This could be someone lost in thought.

There is also a power gaze, a short and intense gaze which can force your will on another person, without being aggressive.

It is not easy to conceal a gaze, since humans are skilled at identifying where fellow humans are looking. This explains why humans, in contrast to other animals, have large eye whites since they help with nonverbal communication.

This is an area that rats liars out. Since they feel guilty when looking at others, they will hardly maintain eye contact. If they, however, know of this, they could even look at you longer than usual, overcompensating for it. There is no definite acceptable duration of gaze, as it varies with culture.

In shopping for items, people usually stare at the options before them, running their eyes over the goods as they scan them. However, people do look longer at whatever piques their interest. Even while they scan others, their gaze will often return to that item. This is a skill that could make all the difference in a sales career.

Glancing

We glance at what we desire, just like glancing at the door could mean that someone is interested in leaving.

Glancing at a person could mean an interest in having a conversation with such a person. You could also glance at someone as a show of concern when a statement that could hurt the person is made.

Glancing could also indicate attraction when you glance sideways at someone with a raised eyebrow. When this is done without a raised eyebrow, it could signal disapproval.

Darting Eyes

This could be an indication of someone feeling insecure. This person might be looking for an excuse or a distraction to avoid conversation.

Eye Contact: Things to Note

Eye contact could lead to more eye contact: Although, many people could be reluctant to initiate eye contact due to the assumption that the other party might not welcome it. Initiate the move, even though the other party might look way at first. By the next move, they might return the gaze. However, if they keep avoiding direct contact after two or three times, it is best you desist.

Avoid being creepy: When you make eye contact the right way, you can use it to convey the right message. When your eye contact is, however, not welcomed, the constant effort could be upsetting. This is because the other person can sense your gaze even when not looking directly at you.

Switch from eye to eye: Let your focus be on one eye for a while, then gradually move to the other eye. This should not be turned into darting, however, as it could be distracting. Slowly alternating between each eye gives the intention that you are paying attention.

Avoid being too obvious: Locking eyes for the whole conversation period is not always a good idea; it is slightly creepy. Look away for a bit.

When breaking a gaze, don't look down: Looking down when you break a gaze could send a wrong message of submission. Rather, look sideways.

Breaking eye contact

As indicated above, continuous eye contact can be intimidating, which makes it essential to break eye contact frequently.

However, people also do break eye contact when they feel uncomfortable, like when something disturbing or insulting was said. Also, when a person experiences personal discomfort, there could be a break in eye contact.

A classic flirtation action is when someone makes and breaks eye contact almost immediately, primarily when the head is held low, signaling submission.

Extensive Eye Contact

When eye contact is held too long, there are several meanings it conveys.

Of course, during active listening sessions, eye contact increases significantly, especially when our attention is caught up by the conversation. Visual thinkers, however, might make less eye contact, as they tend to stare upward as they try to visualize the subject of discussion.

People also tend to look more at those they find attractive. It is a confirmed sign of attraction when accompanied by a smile and doe eyes. This explains why lovers like gazing into each other's eyes.

Women also tend to hold the other person's gaze for three seconds or so. After this, she looks down for a second or two and looks up again. This is to determine if the other person is still looking at them. If they are, they return a slight smile that indicates that "yes, I was hoping for this." This is an attraction signal common to women.

Excessive eye contact can be unnerving. You can reduce stress from this by making contact with the bridge of the nose. The other party still thinks you are looking at their eyes.

Eye Contact in Persuasion

Eye contact is the key to persuasion. When discussing something with someone and they do not return your gaze, they are probably thinking about another thing, with divided attention. The personal connection is not there even if they can hear you.

Eye contact is essential in persuasion; hence, you want to achieve and sustain this if you are trying to persuade someone.

Staring

Staring is done by looking at someone or something for a pretty long time with the eyes wide open. It is done with reduced blinking and signifies a particular interest in the person or thing.

Staring could also signal disbelief or shock after a piece of sudden news.

When staring is, however, done with a defocused eye, the person might be lost in thought and the thing or person they are staring at will not be relevant in any way.

A short stare could also indicate surprise when done with the eyes opened wide and then returned quickly to normal. The return back to normal might be because the person suddenly realizes how impolite it will be to stare.

The acceptable length with which it is okay to stare varies due to culture. Babies and young ones often stare until they get to learn cultural values.

Final Thoughts

As evident from this section, there is much more that you can tell about a person from their eyes. The eye direction, the pattern of movement, and more all carry significant meaning and messages that might give insight into the mind of the person.

The eyes are indeed the windows to the soul - not only the soul, but the mind as well.

Chapter 3
Detecting Specific Personality Traits through Body Language

Immediately when we meet people, we are unconsciously drawing conclusions about them. This is a trait that is built into everyone, as we rely on these assumptions to go through life and relate well with others. A knowledge of DISC and the associated body language peculiar to each helps make a better judgment that you can refine as you get to know the person.

Your personality says a lot about you and how you do things. How you talk, stand, move, eat, and your gestures reveal a lot more about you than you realize. Also, with a good understanding of body language, you can decide someone's personality by analyzing their paralanguage.

With a good understanding of body language, you can know the best way to interact with anyone based on that body language. It can help you build rapport and foster connections.

Using the DISC personality as a guide, you can ascertain and associate some specific body language that distinguishes the four personality types. DISC is a personality assessment that was introduced by William Moulton Marston, Ph.D., an expert in personality and body language (Marston, 1979).

According to him, the four personality types are:

- The Driver who wants to "Get Things Done."
- The Influencer who wants to "Be Appreciated."
- The Supporter who wants to "Flow Along."
- The Careful Corrector who wants "Things Done Right."

Analyzing Various Personality Types

The Driver - Get it Done

The body language cues from the Driver are strong and confident. They appear commanding, authoritative, and will bond easily when they enter a room. They make strong and direct eye contact. They talk fast, loud, and forcefully. They do not mind interrupting when passing their message across. They are not the type to beat around the bush, as they love to be quick and straight to the point.

They make quick decisions and also value brevity. In communicating with them, get straight to the point. They're not fans of details and excessive repetition. If you want to give them a call or send an email, you had better go straight to the point.

They are the type that multitasks even though nothing excites them as much as getting the task done.

In tackling long term or detailed project, they perform better by breaking this down into small milestones. Their philosophy is to get things done and face the next challenge. Being in charge and combating challenge fuels them. They exude intense, challenging, forceful, and commanding body language. In relating with them, you had better know what you want and stick to it. They appreciate and respond to confident body language, direct eye contact, and a strong and fast voice.

The Influencer – Get Appreciated

You can quickly know this type, as they are the expressive speaker. They wear a cheerful smile and are charismatic. They tend to engage others with their voice and they are the type that often gesticulates, talking with their hands, and expressing themselves with their whole body. You can easily decode what is going on with them via their expressive facial language. They are enthusiastic and laugh easily.

They seem to always have fun, talk, and move fast as well as keep their heart opened. They seem to be happy people who also want others to be happy and excited. They love taking on challenges and every opportunity to learn. As a result of this, they will easily take on a new project because it is unique. However, they get bored easily, which stems from the fact that they love new things. This is one of their shortcomings, as they might not see the new project they took to completion.

Since they get bored quickly, they are not good with projects that require many minute details or multiple complicated steps.

To get them to perform better at a job that requires intricate details, you have got to provide them with social interaction, some form of motivation, etc. They are lively people, hence to flow with them you have to be energetic as well. They enjoy a good sense of humor; they love new directions, beautiful ideas, and innovation.

Since they are expressive, they love leading and influencing others. You can engage them by giving them an assignment where they get to bring others onboard. If your project interests them, there is a high probability it will be a success. They thrive on being the center of attention. They love being appreciated as well, as it keeps them motivated. In relating to an influencer, you have got to be energetic and present energetic and open body language.

The Supporters – Get Along

These can be said to be the pillars which are working behind the scene to keep things going smoothly. They are relaxed, friendly, and warm. They present a steady and stable smile. They do not talk fast, unlike the previous two personalities; instead, they speak slowly and thoughtfully.

People will likely refer to a supporter as a good listener, even though, at times, supporters feel that no one gives them the chance to talk. However, they do not mind being interrupted and offer a listening ear when another person needs them. Supporters are known for revealing great listening body language. They are the empathic type that will show sympathetic facial expressions, and they will nod their head and lean in.

They are pretty helpful and nurturing towards others. They are meticulous, as little details count. Since they are warm, they will often reach out, smile, hug, and shake hands. They value warmhearted, friendly, and relaxed conversation. In relating with them, take an interest in their weekend and their family, as they appreciate this.

In contrast to the two personalities discussed above, they do not take any action until they have given it deep thought. They are not a big fan of change; hence, you have to simplify any new project you want to give them. If not, they will instead subscribe to the old ways of doing things which have always worked for them. In relating with a supporter, be a friend. Present a warm body language alongside a sweet, relaxed, and soft voice, with a smile of course.

The Careful Corrector - Get it Right

Even though they like to solve the problem and get to the root of any situation, they often present reserved body language. You will often see them with their hands behind their back or in their pockets. They are usually thinking and go about with a facial expression that's pretty hard to decode.

They will present a thinking body language - thumb on the chin and the forefingers up. They typically converse with a low pitched voice at a slow pace. Compared to Drivers and Influencers, they sound monotone. Even though they feel things deeply, they could appear to others as cold and unemotional.

They are very organized, smart, and analytical. They hardly talk until they have something to say. They prefer to have the facts and the specific words to say before voicing their opinions.

Final Thoughts

Even without knowing anything about someone, you can pay attention to the patterns of behaviors and body cues to determine the personality type. This knowledge can set you apart in your relationship and workplace and help you make a correct impression about someone that you can use to your advantage.

Chapter 4
Detecting Lies and Deception

Signs Someone is Lying

The signs that someone is lying are not always easy to decipher. On the other hand you cannot always conclude that someone is sincere. This, however, boils down to trusting your instinct. In detecting a lie, some telltale signs could identify a liar. Watch out for the following signs, among others.

It is important to note that you need to be careful of the lying signal you are basing your conclusion on. As established in some chapters above, shifty eyes could mean someone in deep thought. Hence, make sure you understand the particular body language sign you are going with. Also, keep in mind that these signs should only be seen as possible indicators and not definite proof that someone is lying. The next section will help give some accurate methods to detect a liar.

Here are some signs of lying:

Changes in Breathing Pattern

Heavy breathing is a reflex action that could indicate that someone is lying. Not only will they breathe heavily, but there could also be a change in breathing pattern. When someone is lying or withholding information, they get nervous, which is seen in the way they breathe. This is a reflex because when people lie, their heart rate and rate of blood flow change, which affects breathing patterns. This also explains why someone lying might have trouble speaking, since the mucous membrane in part of the mouth dries out.

They Desperately Try to Be Still

When humans get nervous, they fidget easily. However, trying to be still could be suspicious. Think about it: people generally are relaxed, free, and open when engaging in normal conversation. These are unconscious body movements that you hardly take note of.

However, when someone presents a rigid stance, there is a big chance that something is off. This might be due to the effort of the person to hide tension by reducing body movement.

Providing Excessive Information

A liar will often give too much information than asked for. The details are usually in excess, all in a bid to try and convince themselves, and you, that they are telling the truth.

Part of what you have to do in trying to get a liar to spill out information is pause. They are not comfortable with silence; hence, you will find them blabbing and blabbing, trying desperately to come up with stories to support their claim.

Difficulty Speaking

If you are interrogating a guilty party, the more he or she cooks up a story, the more difficult it becomes for the person to speak. This is due to the stress that is placed on the autonomic nervous system. As a result of this, there tends to be a decrease in the rate of flow of saliva to the mouth

Excessive Staring

A liar will often try to avoid eye contact. On the other hand, they might go the extra mile and maintain excessive eye contact. This is usually in an attempt to manipulate and control you. If someone has an honest conversation, they will be comfortable breaking eye contact once in a while. Liars, on the other hand, might try to overcompensate by giving a cold, steady gaze.

Be sure to watch out for excessive blinking as well.

Watch out for Excessive Pauses

Unusual and excessive pauses are a clear sign that something is off. This could be a smart way to buy time to gather the thought and come up with a storyline to present to you. Look for, and take note of, these pauses. You will see them hesitating, appearing to be thinking hard. These are tactics to try to construct a believable story.

Watch out for Fidgeting

Fidgeting is a nervous reaction, a clear indication of negative energy. Most liars, except psychopaths, of course, do fall victim to this. Since they are not sure you will buy their story or not, they tend to resort to various means to let go of the negative energy. Hence, you see them play with their thumbs, stroke their hair, bite their lip, or tap their feet.

Feet shuffling, for instance, is a sign that the body is taking over. It is a clear sign they are not comfortable and want to leave. Watch out for this sign.

Repeating the Question

In a bid to get their story right and make sure their facts do not contradict each other, a liar could stall for time. This might be an effort to dig deeper and know how much of the truth you know. This, alongside other clues, could help you tell if someone is lying. Do not rule out the possibility that someone might want to make sure they heard you correctly.

How to Know if Someone is Lying to You

You do not have to be a top CIA profiler to detect a lie. Part of our aim in this book is to equip you with useful, practical lie detection skills. There is always the chance that you are getting lied to more often than you are aware. How beautiful would it be if you could detect deception in your life, business, and relationships?

Absence of this skill is like leaving the fate of your life to chance. Just like any skill, you can learn lie detection and develop the ability over time. We are going to divide the process of lie detection into three parts:

- Part 1: Establish the norms
- Part 2: Look for deviation from the baselines and other lying clues
- Part 3: If you suspect a lie, press further

The rest of this chapter will shed light on each point above. Once you are done, you will be confident of your lie detection skills and that no one will be able to deceive you again.

Part 1: Establish the Norms

Also called baseline, this is the typical behavior of a person under normal conditions; in other words, when they have no reason to lie. This is the foundation of everything, a crucial part.

In establishing this, be sure to try and build rapport with the person. This happens by engaging them in a conversation where they reveal facts or information about themselves willingly, without any need to lie. You could discuss the weather, ask after their favorite celebrity, politics, etc. While at this, be sure to take note of how they sound, how they talk, their choice of words, etc. We start with the physical norms.

Part 1a: The Physical Norms

To establish the physical baseline, take note of the physical characteristics of various part of their body while they are talking freely. We break this down based on the different parts of the body. Be sure to consider the:

Face

Head

Torso

Arms and hands

Legs and feet

Your job here is to keep tabs on various parts of the body and their behaviors during normal conversation. Do they stroke their hair? Do they cover their mouth? Are they playing with their sleeve button? Are they gesticulating? These are very important in establishing the physical baseline.

It does not stop at that. We want to establish strong evidence that someone is lying, so we also consider the audio norms.

Part 1b: The Audio Model

This is where you take note of how they sound and their choice of words during regular communication, when they have no reason to lie. Do they pause while talking? Do they talk fast? Do they talk slow? What is the tone and volume they use? Is there anything unusual in their speech patterns? What about umm and ahhs?

It does not stop here, as you have to establish their characteristics in normal conversation that could be quite upsetting. With this, you can look for discrepancies in determining a lie.

The emotional norm is their characteristics when they are upset, excited, anxious, or nervous about something. This will help you get a solid baseline so you do not pass off someone who is only nervous or upset as lying. This is a flaw of many lie detectors. They assume the person is lying, whereas they are just emotional about the subject.

Part 1c: Emotional Baseline

While this also involves questions or conversations, they should be questions that will either get the person excited or upset. With this, you get to establish the physical and audio norms when they are emotional.

This is not the time to discuss politics, but rather a cause that's going to get them excited or upset. Did they lose a lot of money in a bet? Capitalize on this. Did they lose an important family member to cancer? Ask about it. Were they wrongly accused and dismissed from work? Ask them about it. Is one of their kids in jail? Bring it up.

With this, you now have a standard, complete character model of your subject. You also have clues that indicate when they are excited or upset about something. These behaviors will stand out when they are lying.

They could stroke their thumb when you bring up an upsetting subject or have a change in volume. Take note. After completing these three exercises, you have a complete baseline process. This has given you a good idea of how the person talks and behaves when there is no reason to lie.

Part 2: Look for Deviation from the Norms

After establishing a norm, the next critical step is to continue your interrogation to determine if the person is lying. Consider it a red flag if they start gesticulating, something they didn't do while you were establishing the norm.

If they start stroking their palm or their hair, it is a sure red flag. It is a red flag as well if their speech suddenly becomes monotone or their volume is too high or low, which is far different from how they talked while establishing the norms.

You have to be attentive to spot these sorts of deviations. In addition to paying attention to these differences, be sure to take note of the signs of lying discussed above. Should there be any of the lying signs presented in the previous section, it is a red flag worth noting. Common examples are:

- Facial emotions that contradict words said
- Touching the mouth or the nose
- Any self-soothing behavior like grooming
- Blocking the ears or mouth when talking and other distancing behavior
- Phrases like 'to be honest' or 'with all sincerity.'
- The appearance of thinking deeply when the conversation doesn't warrant much thought

As you progress with the conversation, or should I say interrogation, you should have noticed variations from the established baseline and other lying cues. Be sure to keep them in mind.

Part 2b: Look for Clusters

In other words, look for two or three various signs of lying or deviations from the norms you have established. As you discuss further, you will detect these clusters. You should not pass someone off as lying without clusters. In other words, having only one sign of lying might not necessarily mean that the person is lying.

Should you have clusters for a particular subject, the person could either be lying, hiding information, or uncomfortable about the issue of discussion. Whatever the case, you should press further.

Part 3: Press Further

If you find two or more of the signs of lying, we recommend that you dig further. However, it is also essential to determine what matters. Every passing day, people lie to each other. Some types of lies are harmless, meant to protect one's feelings, and if it doesn't matter, you have to let it go.

Consider a wife asking her husband, "Honey, do I look fat?" If the man respond honestly, it could break the wife's heart, and her mood becomes dampened. If the husband knows this, he could lie and say no. This way, he saves himself the headache of dealing with an emotional wife and having to console her.

However, if it is essential you know the truth, you can press further. There are many ways you can dig deeper.

You can ask them to tell the story in reverse, that is, from the end. This is mentally taxing, and you will often see a liar struggling to be coherent.

You could also employ open-ended questions like, "I would love to know more about…" Or, "When you said this, what did you mean?" With this, they have no choice but to talk more, exposing their vulnerability. You can also throw them off balance by asking an unexpected question. With this, you get to watch their reaction destabilize them now that the story they cooked up will be of no use.

Final Thoughts

Detecting a lie is as simple as this. It is essential, however, to give yourself the chance to get better with time. This is a valuable skill that takes time to develop.

Also, bear in mind that there is no shortcut to identifying a liar. While the skill could take time to develop, you get to save yourself, your relationships, and your loved ones. All in all, you make smarter decisions and create deeper, more meaningful relationships.

Chapter 5
Signals of Attraction: How to Know if Someone Likes You

Okay, let's say you are at a party and you spot someone you are interested in. You summon up the courage to walk up to them and strike up a conversation. As mentioned, you took an interest in them, but you are not sure if they share the same feelings. In trying to maintain your dignity, you left the conversation without making a move.

Does this sound familiar? Many people are clueless about picking up on signs of attraction. If you are in this category, this chapter will guide you and help you learn to spot attraction and go after it.

Surefire Signs of Male Attraction

To determine if a man likes you, here are some signs to look for:

Uninterrupted Eye Contact

To determine if a man is interested in you, his eyes will often give clues. You will often catch him stealing glances at you if he's genuinely interested in you. Besides, we have established in previous chapters that if someone is attracted to another person, the pupils will dilate. Watch out for physical changes in the pupil size.

He will put forward his best foot

A man genuinely interested in you will reveal evident confidence while talking to you, provided he is not the shy type. They might puff out their chest or flex their muscle while talking to you. They might stand up straight and tall, in a bid to make their stature look bigger while talking to you. In short, you will see them emphasize parts of their body they are proud of.

He gets closer and talks to you confidently

When we are attracted to anyone, all we want to do at that moment is get their attention and maintain it for as long as we can. Hence, the manner of conversation of a man genuinely interested in a woman will be unique. Watch out for conversations that focus on you and what you love, conversations that keep the spotlight on you and make you feel good about yourself.

Generally, people love it when they are the center of attention. If you have this kind of conversation with a man, there is a good chance that he is attracted to you.

You will Notice a Couple of Your Quirks in His Actions

Someone who genuinely likes you will unconsciously mimic your verbal and body language. You will see them using a particular word or phrase you often use, even though they had not used it before. He might also try and mirror your body language!

Other signs of attraction that you will see from a man who is into you are:

- An eyebrow flash which often happens subconsciously
- Parted lips that happen when your eyes meet
- Flared nostrils
- Self-grooming that happens unconsciously, like smoothing or stroking his hair
- Standing directly before you, tall with a wide stance
- He might spread his legs to show his asset if he's sitting
- He could adjust his package if he's standing
- If wearing a jacket, he plays with the buttons

Surefire Signs of Female Attraction

Just like men, there are signs that a woman displays when she takes an interest in a man. Some of these are:

Peacocking

The same way a man will reveal his physical assets that he is proud of to someone he has an interest in, a woman will also show forth her best physical assets to try and get a man's attention. Notice if the lady is playing with her hair or adjusting her clothes. The manner she does it in matters, as she could just be trying to fix something.

She Laughs a Lot

A woman that is attracted to you will laugh whether your jokes are funny or not. Capitalize on this by saying something mildly amusing. Did she give a chuckle, or a laugh like it was hilarious? Pay attention, as you get to judge if she is into you.

She is After Deep Conversation

You can have a general conversation with anyone about who they are and their life in general. If you, however, try to press for in-depth discussions and she does not resist, there is a big chance she is interested in you. She will also show genuine interest in getting to know more about you.

Her Voice gets Higher When Speaking

A man tends to talk at a low register when talking to the one he likes. A woman, on the other hand, projects her voice. Be sure to take note of her voice. If it is possible, examine how she talks to others and compare it to how she talks to you. Is there a difference in the tone? If her manner of talking to you differs from others, other men included, there is a big chance she is attracted to you.

Other subtle signs from a lady that likes a man are:

- Licking her lips and pouting while gazing towards the man
- Shows off her hip by standing with a hip slightly thrust forward
- Looks sideways with a slightly raised shoulder which emphasizes her breasts
- Displaying the wrist, a delicate part of their body
- The ankles will be crossed in a bid to make the hips wider and legs slimmer. This will also subconsciously point the knees at him
- Looking at the man with her hands on her chin subconsciously asking: "Here is my face, do you find it attractive?"
- Accidental or intentional touching

It is essential to establish that these are mere signs and not a certainty. Also, examine the context before assuming someone is attracted to you.

Attraction and Associated Body Language

We dedicated this chapter to teaching you how to decide if someone is attracted to you or not. You can improve your chances by arming yourself with sure-fire tips from body language. Humans communicate messages consciously and unconsciously.

Many times, our body unconsciously puts forth some distinctive signs when we are attracted to another person. The knowledge of these body language signs is critical and essential. It can help determine if someone genuinely likes you or not. You also get to assess the level of your present relationship and ascertain if your partner really is in love with you or not.

Analyzing the Body Language of Attraction

Basically, the messages that attraction body language passes are:

- I am interested
- I come in peace
- You can talk to me
- I am fertile

While it does not sound very romantic, it is a critical part of the human mating experience. If your body language reveals unavailability, other people, and potential mates, will pick up on that and let you be.

The way body language works is unique and mysterious. There is a direct form of communication between the brain and our body, all beyond our conscious thought. As a result of this, when you find someone attractive, the body in turn sends out a physical signal in response to such attraction.

This is why we tend to lean towards those we are attracted to, which signifies interest and engagement; in contrast, when we lean away, we are withdrawing.

When you tilt your head towards someone, there is a big chance you are interested in that person. However, avoiding eye contact sends a message of lack of interest. So if you like someone, even if you are shy, be sure to use eye contact to your advantage.

Another unconscious response that shows you are attracted to someone is a racing heart. If you are near someone you are attracted to, your heartbeat quickens.

There are two dominant primary body language signs of attraction: Mirroring and Blushing.

Mirroring: A Sign of Attraction

Mirroring is one of the positive indications that someone is attracted to something or someone. Hence, once you notice this, know that they are either attracted to you or the exact thing they are mirroring. For instance, if someone bites their lips and you find it strangely interesting, you could subconsciously bite your lips as well in a bid to look attractive, like the person you are mirroring.

Have it in mind that the person who mirrors feels a strong admiration and connection with the person they are imitating. This explains why mirroring is a sure sign of attraction.

Blushing: A Sign of Attraction

Blushing is to the face as an orgasm is to the sexual organs. It is an involuntary action that signals interest and availability. Here are four points that explain why people blush before the person they are attracted to:

Admiration: In other words, you feel the person you are attracted to is the best on the entire Earth. You feel proud of your choice, which is revealed via blushing.

Eagerness: How we wait for their message, their call, or even a longing touch. Upon getting whatever it is that your heart has so longed for, your joy knows no bounds.

Anxiety: But not the bad kind. Have you heard of butterflies in the stomach? These awesome creatures make people blush.

Sudden eye-contact: Eye contact with someone you are attracted to can trigger feelings of embarrassment. When this happens, your cheeks will tell on you.

The body, which does not lie, does an excellent job of betraying us. Your body can indicate if you are attracted to someone or not. These subtle signs will let you know without any doubt.

Chapter 6
How to Know You are Insecure

Everyone struggles with some level of insecurity which stems from things you do not like about yourself. As a result, failure to confront and deal with things about you that do not please you could position you for a serious problem.

When someone is insecure, you will see some sure signs like poor social skills and withdrawn body language. Aside from this, there are also many signs that do not relate to insecurity. In fact, there are behaviors associated with confidence, yet if you look deeper, have insecurity written all over them.

With this in mind, how do you determine if you are insecure? We have here many signs with which you can gauge yourself and know if you are insecure or not. Mind you, displaying these behaviors does not necessarily point to self-doubt. However, it is important to understand what these behaviors mean.

All in all, it is natural to feel some level of insecurity. Your manner of dealing with it makes the difference. Watch out for the following signs:

You Put Yourself Down

It is common knowledge that if you are not sure of yourself or your ability, you will likely always put yourself down. For a couple of days, take note of your body language and how often you make comments about yourself. It could amaze you. Many people do not realize how often they fail themselves at the task. You hear statements like: 'I am not good at this.'

Would you make these derogatory remarks to someone you care about? Your answer should be no, and if it is, then you are worthy of self love. You do not have to be so hard on yourself. It is not modesty. Many people find it easy to make fun of themselves when they are insecure. They conclude that laughing at themselves will not make it a big deal, especially when others do as well.

Watch it!

You Put Others Down

You are not as confident as you think you are if you are always trying to make others feel bad about themselves. Okay, we understand that it takes a lot of guts to say something cruel about someone, but the real question is why must you be the bearer of bad news? There is a big chance you are probably doing this to make yourself feel better; one of the signs of insecurity!

Whereas, if you feel good about yourself, there will be no need to make others feel bad. Be careful of this, as it happens when insecurity is coming between you and the ones you care about. Hence, if you always say mean things to others, there might be another underlying issue. Feelings of inadequacy can be managed in mature ways that don't involve insults!

You are Hardly Happy for Others

Almost everyone with a feeling of insecurity will manifest this trait! How can you be happy for someone else if you are not first happy with yourself and who you are? If you like or love someone, you should always be after the best for them. There's always the chance that you'll be a little jealous if they got a new job, won the lottery, or received something you have been after for years - and that's okay.

However, there is a difference between jealousy and being toxic. You can be jealous and be happy for someone. Yet, if it upsets you that people in your life experience good things, you may have issues with insecurity.

You Hide Things About Your Life

If you find it difficult to let people in on some areas of your life, there is a big chance you are insecure. Without a doubt, there is the place of privacy in which some things are not for public consumption. However, when there is no real reason to keep anything secret, yet you find it difficult to let people in, there is a chance you are embarrassed about it.

You might lie to your friend about the grades you got in college, the kind of job you do, etc. This, of course, spells out insecurity. There is no point in being embarrassed about a part of your life that is not what people expected it to be like. Bear in mind that being afraid to let people in on things you are embarrassed about means you are being hard on yourself, much harder than others will be.

You Like Being the Center of Attraction

Say you want to help people, and in doing so, you bring up things about you. People might accept this as confidence, which might be right. However, it could also point out insecurity. Think about it: attempting to bring yourself into every conversation points to one thing – you are probably always thinking about yourself. This could mean you are thinking about how amazing you are and you just have to flaunt it. You are always analyzing yourself, and you care about how you appear to others.

If you are always bringing things about yourself and your life into conversations, it might be your subconscious craving for attention. This is because you feel your personal approval and opinions are not good enough; hence, the validations of others matters.

Interestingly, on the other end of the scale, if you hate being the center of attention and you try to change the subject when people talk about you, it might also be insecurity. In other words, you feel you are not so important as to be discussed.

You Tend to Push people Away

It is understandable that you might have to let go of some people when you do not like them or they don't add to your life in a meaningful way. When it, however, becomes a habit such that you cannot get close to anyone, it could be your insecurity on the loose. You might assume you are not worthy of attention, or you dread someone taking advantage of you, or you feel you do not deserve proper treatment.

Bear in mind, however, that people will probably treat you how you treat yourself. Hence, if you do not love yourself or treat yourself well, you cannot expect others to.

You Always Get Defensive

When you get defensive, that is a sure sign that you are fixated on your insecurities rather than your immediate world. This doesn't mean you shouldn't defend yourself when someone says something mean or untrue; in other words, when the need arises. However, taking offense at the slightest provocation, something that is not very offensive, taking something personal when it is not worth the tantrum, indicate the chance that this is your insecurity getting the better of you.

You Tend to be a People Pleaser

A constant need to please people in order to get their approval is a sign that you are insecure. This habit affects your life, as it makes you feel that your life is not yours since you have made it a habit to always get people's approval.

Caring and being compassionate to others is different from trying to please people. People without insecurities understand this, and they know that they do not hold the key to other people's happiness, which is true. You are not obligated to rescue everyone from every unpleasant experience.

Be sure to try and do things that make you happy. Make room in your life to attend to your goals and what will bring your dreams to fruition as well.

You Tend to be a Perfectionist

If you devote an extensive amount of time to getting things done right, or you feel your efforts are not good enough no matter what, you might be insecure. Many times, the underlying factor is a fear of failure or criticism. As a result, you will instead remain at a project or a job due to fear of what the future, the outcome, holds.

The effect of this is evident; you get stuck and don't make any meaningful progress. Or, you devote an excessive amount of time to everything you commit yourself to. With this, you do not meet deadlines, and you might also let people down.

Perfectionism is a disease that can be hard to let go of. However, you have to be kind to yourself and also accept who you are.

You Have a Temper

Anger issues could be an indication that you do not feel great about yourself. In fact, anger as a response might be a subconscious way of diverting attention from your personal flaws and insecurities. You think that if you do this, you get to feign a tough exterior, scaring people away from getting to know the real you.

On the other hand, you might be angry about the thing that makes you deficient. You might not be able to stop yourself from taking this anger out on other people around you. Being angry all the time is really not a good thing. If you have anger issues, there is a big chance there is an underlying cause that is getting on your nerves.

Final Thoughts

As you can see, it is evident from this chapter that many behaviors reveal insecurity as the main cause. It takes digging deeper to know that the underlying cause is insecurity and to address it. Compare the behaviors discussed to your habits and lifestyle, and you can confirm if you are the victim of insecurity or not.

Chapter 7
How to Influence People

There is no single way of influencing people. Everyone is capable of influencing and being influenced. Every one of us is influenced by places, people, situations, and events.

In our workplace as well, we are subject to influencing and being influenced by people. Influence can take on various forms. It could be in the form of inspiring others, engaging people's imagination, and persuading others. All in all, being a good influencer makes your life easy.

If you can effectively use your influencing skill, it will be easy for you to gain the interest and trust of others. People who can influence others do not sit, complain, and wait for things to happen. They have the zeal to go after what needs to be done and get it done.

For your influencing skills to be effective, they have to involve a healthy mix of communication, presentation, assertiveness, and interpersonal techniques. In other words, you can adjust your personal style when you know of the type of effect you have on others, without changing who you are.

Influencing People vs. Coercion and Manipulation

Of course, you might succeed in dominating people via coercion and manipulation. It could even help you get things done. It is, however, different from influencing people. It is tantamount to forcing people to do what you want. While you might make them go against their will, you will hardly have their support.

Forcing people against their will to do anything will leave them with a horrible impression about you. They will hold onto this impression, which might be pretty difficult to change unless you change your approach.

As a general rule, when people feel valued, acknowledged, or appreciated, they will likely go the extra mile for you. You could get them to do something they don't want to do since they now feel good about their choice.

How to Influence People

For you to influence people the right way, you have to understand yourself and the kind of impact you have on others. In other words, the kind of impression other people have of you must change.

Irrespective of what you have going on in your mind, if the other person or your audience does not perceive it, it only exists in your head.

This explains why you could give a speech you thought was fantastic. However, if your audience doesn't follow you, you are the only one that will consider the speech as a success.

Some thoughtful ways to influence people are:

Respond, Don't React

It is usual for people to flare up and react when we or something we care about is attacked. We have all been in such a situation. Taking a moment to breathe and regain your composure in such a moment is vital. The few seconds of pause will help you react objectively, allowing you to respond effectively.

Responding differs from reaction, because it takes emotion out of the situation. Besides, it shows others how powerful you are, since you can keep your emotions in check. It helps you look at the situation objectively and bring out positivity.

When Things Go Wrong, Stay Neutral

Life is not a bed of roses. Life comes with good and bad times, happy and sad moments. While we all hope everything remains positive and smooth, it hardly happens this way. However, being able to journey through all life throws at you with hope and positivity is pretty vital.

Life will come with some daunting events, but your ability to remain neutral will radiating a positive influence will be beneficial. This is more helpful and more mature than being emotional and subjective.

Give People What They Want

When influencing people, it is no longer about you and what you want, but about them. Hence, what they wish for matters because that will make an impact on them, not what you want.

Get yourself out of the spotlight for a moment. Prioritizing what others want will make you indispensable, and you will earn their respect.

Make People Feel Important

As long as you can make people feel important, valued, and wanted, they will go out of their way for you. This is the most essential factor in influencing people.

Everyone, including you, likes to feel important. You can use this to your advantage. Making people do what they don't feel like doing isn't possible - unless you have some kind of influence on them.

A janitor, for instance, might go about their daily job because they have to. However, if they feel valued, part of something bigger, they will be passionate about what they do.

Be Sincere About Your Emotions

In influencing others, you are not to deny or ignore your own emotions even if they are negative. On the contrary, it means you are mature enough to get in touch and take positive actions to heal. Many people are fond of passing the blame on others, yet we are all responsible for our emotions. No one, without your permission, can make you feel bad.

Respect People's Opinions

People do not have to share the same opinion as you, and the fact that their opinion differs does not mean they are wrong. It is rude to pass their judgment off as wrong.

Even if they are wrong, your choice of words matters a lot. Let them know you do not agree with them, but don't attack their ideas. That is the best way to disagree without offending their self-esteem.

Final Thoughts

You do not have to be a leader before you learn the art of influencing people. Making a few positive changes to your behavior and attitude will translate positively to other people around. Besides, when you carry a positive aura with you, it will be reflected in your actions and emotions, which will surely be transferred to people around you.

Chapter 8
Powerful Tips on How to Read People

The art of reading people is a crucial and vital skill. It's no wonder security agencies like the FBI and CIA employ specialists to do this. The good news is that you do need to be an FBI profiler before you can read people.

From understanding eye movement and contact to reading body language and emotional intelligence – you are capable of reading people. It is essential to emphasize at this junction that reading people is a skill humans are naturally wired with. Every time you interact with people, you are reading them.

With that aside, with practice, you can develop your people reading skills.

Why is it important to know how to read people?

The interaction of various people at a time is essential to the survival of man. The ability to decide when not to interact with others is also vital. Also, the better you can read people, the more you can get from them.

Reading People Naturally

As established above, nature has built the skill to understand people in us all. When interacting with people, you automatically do the following:

- You are evaluating them subconsciously. You access their appearance, body language, and behavior. You try to understand their motives and intentions.
- You are also reading them consciously. In other words, you are evaluating their appearance, motives, and body language. In any interaction, you will probably take into account a couple of things about the person you are talking to.
- You appropriately respond to them based on your assessment. This happens after you have subconsciously evaluated the person.

This is the basic form in which all human interaction takes place.

As an example, let us assume some random guy walks up to you and greets you in a friendly manner. Instantly, your brain assesses his style of dress and evaluates him as well dressed, and nothing about him seems off or suspicious.

You might not think about it consciously, but your subconscious is busy doing the evaluation. After assessing him, you return his greeting with a hello. This was the response of your assessment of him (his body language, voice, appearance, etc.).

This shows that to read people, the conscious thought plays a significant role as well. You may subconsciously be assessing them while consciously drawing conclusions from those assessments.

Another example is that you might be at a party sitting in a corner by yourself. Your eyes are traveling around the length and breadth of the room, consciously evaluating the people and assessing potential threats. Your subconscious continually takes in the information from your conscious and does it's own check to ensure you're safe. Those "feelings" you get about certain people or places come from your subconscious assessment.

How to Read People

The idea behind these examples is that we all read people naturally, although some people are better at it than others. You can, however, develop your skill of reading people by learning from books (like this) or in a classroom.

We have examined various ways to read people's body language in the early part of this chapter. This is very important to get better at your job or improve your relationship. However, without any prior lesson or knowledge on body language, you can figure out what someone's body language is saying via instinct.

Let's proceed to the basic tips on reading people:

Understand the Basic Needs of People

In learning how to read people, an understanding of Maslow's Hierarchy of Needs is very important. Although not a perfect model, it does teach a lot of practical concepts in human psychology. How people behave, alongside their motives, is determined by their utmost needs and desires. Maslow explains that these needs come from a ground-up approach (Wikipedia, 2019).

In other words, people will act based on their needs, what they want. This could, however, depend on the circumstance, type of need, level of desperation, and personality type. A hungry person, for instance, might just need to fix a meal in the kitchen or walk up to a restaurant. If they don't have money, they might rob or maim another person to get money to fulfill this need. This is where desperation, circumstance, and personality come to play.

We can group the needs of people in various ways. In general, however, after psychological needs come safety needs. If a person does not feel secure, there will be an outburst of emotions like anxiety and fear, which could drive them to look for security.

After this comes love. People look for affection and relationship security after the first two needs are handled.

Next is esteem needs. In other words, it allows a person to satisfy their ego and give their life meaning. While it is not required for living, it helps make life better.

Human behavior generally revolves around these needs. You

can see this evident when people act emotionally. Hence, in reading someone, be sure to determine the need and then respond appropriately.

If you threaten someone's ego, be prepared for a verbal attack, since you have attacked their esteem needs. You have essentially provoked their sense of belonging in the world. They may react mildly or strongly, based on the current emotional state and how much of a threat you are perceived to be.

As another example, someone who perceives that their success at an interview is in jeopardy will likely be very mad at you if you block their car, causing them to be late. This person already ties their safety needs to their success at the interview, therefore anything that stands between them and the job is a threat.

On a final note, bear in mind that motives are what fuel behaviors. Behaviors, on the other hand, are the physical manifestation. Hence, motives trigger behaviors.

Understand Emotional Intelligence

Understanding yourself is crucial to understanding others. To understand yourself, however, you need to develop emotional intelligence. In summary, what is emotional intelligence?

- Self-awareness: the ability to understand your emotions and their impact on your life as a whole.
- Being in touch with your emotions as well as those of others.
- The ability to give the right response to other people's emotions.

You are a rational person with limitations. This is one of the key concepts in developing emotional intelligence. What this means is that your brain evolved from the "ground up." This is also the order in which thoughts appear. Emotions come before higher thought.

Maslow's Hierarchy of Needs revealed this very well. This is why security and physiological needs are at the bottom of the need hierarchy, while self actualization comes first.

The reason is simple - emotions are essential to keep us alive, help us survive, and reproduce. These examples explain this better:

- Fear will keep us away from dangers and threats, even if it prevents us from accomplishing great things
- Anger will help protect our ego and also fight off threats
- Love will help us reproduce and provide for our family and friends
- Anxiety will prepare us for threats, whether real or imagined.

This is the idea, and this is the way our brain has developed, since reproduction and survival are (were) much more important than thinking rationally.

There are times we find ourselves in highly emotional situations which support the fact that emotions are powerful and come before higher thought. An example is a recent breakup. Without a doubt, for the next couple of days, it will take over your thinking. You will be upset and sad, and probably angry as well.

The problem comes when people do not realize their emotions

have taken over yet, and those emotions continue to guide them.

Many people invest in ponzi schemes, for instance, because they were probably driven by emotion. Things might go well until they realize that it is a bad investment and they lose a lot of money. They then realize how excessively optimistic they were, which drove their investment.

This explains how powerful our emotions are, and how they can determine our behavior. This is why working with people's emotions is the best way to influence them.

This is one secret known to great marketers. Marketers know that people rarely base their purchase decision on rationality, so they strive to manipulate and capitalize on their emotions.

People's emotions influence a lot about them and manifest in their actions and daily decisions. Although, some people can be more emotional compared to others. In reading people, identifying the emotion is critical. For instance, if you can identify that someone is:

- Upset, you might not want to make any requests
- Fearful, you could use that to get them to buy something
- Sad, you could try and comfort them

On a final note, whenever you see someone getting emotional, consider Maslow's Hierarchy of Needs. An upset person will have an emotion from the pyramid of needs, and considering this will help you assess the situation well.

Know How to Decode Body Language

Knowing how to read body language is a critical part of reading people. Body language is a broad topic, and hopefully the chapters above have given you an idea of reading body language. In addition, take note of the following:

- If they stand with their chest up, taking a lot of space, with a dominant posture while appearing strong and confident, there is a good chance they are in charge.
- If, while talking, they have their feet pointed away from you, they probably want to leave.
- If it's a woman, consider if she is giving out some signs of attraction as discussed in some chapters above. If yes, she wants to take the interaction further.
- Consider if they are touching themselves excessively. This is in a bid to calm themselves down, as people do this when uncomfortable. It could be the subject of discussion or the person.
- If they are mimicking your body language, you have established rapport.

All in all, consider the overall impression you get from the person. Do you feel they are interested in a conversation, or about to leave? Do they appear to be friendly or a threat? If their behavior or body language shuts you out, they probably do not want to be around.

In considering the body language as well, there is the aspect of reading the person's behavior in context. Is the person's behavior appropriate for the context? Is something about them off? Are they dressed normally?

Another thing about body language as well is that it has to complete the entire picture. In considering their intention, you need to examine what their intention is in relation to the overall body language picture.

It is also important to bear in mind that people could intentionally mislead you with their body language. Someone could cross their arms on purpose or act generally uninterested to mislead you. Someone could be extra nice in a bid to make you feel warmer towards them. Be sure to follow your gut.

Understand How Ego Drives Human Behavior

One of the most powerful driving forces of human thought and action is the ego. Ego is man's need to be respected and relevant in the world around. You see people acting out their ego when you insult them, say something that affects their self image, or even correct them in public.

Hence, anytime someone's ego is threatened, they will act out to try and defend it. No one likes the feeling of being disrespected.

Whatever a person invest their ego in also has a lot to say about them. Called ego investment, it is important and can make the person mad if the investment is attacked, as this is what they take pride in. Some common ego investments are:

- Standing out as an expert in a field
- Distinguishing oneself for a particular positive trait
- A strong cause, belief, or religion
- Social status in life
- Well-being of a group that reflects the person's value

You can understand a lot about someone based on what and where their ego investment lies. Besides, people with lots of personal insecurities will invest their ego in social status.

You can find a lot of people who associate their ego with a local or international sports team. Hence, they take the loss of their team so personal that a sane person will find it abnormal.

The bottom line here is everyone invests their ego in something, even though some people could have theirs in the wrong thing.

Ego is part of the self esteem needs of people, and self esteem needs are above safety and psychological needs. This is why it is a primal instinct in people to defend their ego whenever attacked. An insult is seen as an attack on the ego, and people will do anything to address it.

This is why it is the wrong tactic to insult someone when you're trying to persuade them. If you do, the person will address the insult before giving ears to your persuasion. You also need to be careful of fragile egos. This happens when you insult someone even if it is not your intention.

Be sure to know when people are acting out based on their ego. An idea of this will help you react accordingly. For instance, you can capitalize on their ego in terms of persuasion or negotiations. This is not about insulting them, but rather appealing to their ego investment.

A person excessively invested in a belief will not see any sense in other beliefs, so what you can do is limited. These sorts of people will either have to hit rock bottom before considering another stance or take baby steps.

You can conclude when someone is excessively ego-invested

when their opinions and rationale just do not add up when discussing logical evidence with them. You see them overreact and lash out at you over simple matters.

An idea of this will guide you in the act of reading people better.

Understand the Psychology of Belief

The knowledge of this is also essential in learning how to read people. It could be simple and complex at the same time.

It is simple in that what you perceive as your identity and abilities determines your beliefs, as it's hard to have a belief that will make you accept your weakness.

It is also complex in that it is a combination of self serving thoughts unique to each person. However, you can predict someone's beliefs by examining their values and characteristics. You, however, cannot predict it all.

Changing someone's beliefs is also difficult, though not impossible. It gets harder if the belief has to do with their ego.

Merely considering someone's life will give you an idea of their kind of belief system. This explains why a person that's been an atheist for their entire life will not see sense or believe there is a God somewhere.

The long and short of the story is that the ability to know what people believe in will tell you a lot about them, thus enabling you to read them. Ask probing questions, bring up various subjects of discussion, and you will get a feel for who they are. Their response and stance can give an idea into what they believe in.

The ability to decode someone's belief will let you know who you are dealing with.

Know that People Hide Weakness

As established above, humans are led by emotions. Even though some people do not like to believe that statement, emotions still guide some of our behaviors and decisions. I am referring to emotions again to make a couple of points.

The first is that the person you are interacting with has a direct influence on your emotions. While they might not be strong emotions, talking to someone, anyone, triggers micro-emotions that determine how you interact. The emotions can range from fear to suspicion, frustration, happiness, respect, and so on.

The point, however, is that people can manipulate this. There is a tendency for people to put up a "veil" in order to appear how they want you to perceive them. This happens by manipulating your emotions. They put up appearances and behaviors that mess with your "micro-emotions" which affects your perception of them. Through their appearance, body language, manner of speech or behavior, they might want you to feel they are older, stronger, nicer, etc.

Keep in mind that someone who manipulates your emotions might not be necessarily "bad." However, many people might hide their negative side using this technique. For instance, someone that has a lot to hide could act overconfident or might flaunt their social status, all in a bid to appear better than they are. Here is the loophole: these sorts of people hide their weaknesses and exaggerate their strengths.

As discussed in some chapters above, an insecure person, for instance, could get excessively angry, defensive, or be a perfectionist all in a bid to hide their vulnerabilities from people. Yet, the reason behind this is because they are not satisfied with their lives.

Adversity Will Reveal Character

The ability to see the true character of people is very important in reading people. It is natural to put up a good image when things are well. There is nothing that will stop you from putting up the best side of yourself when you are not threatened by the environment.

However, the real test of character comes when emotions and adversities arise. The real character of most people comes out when they get emotional. While some people can control their emotions well, many people tend to be in-between, and others have poor control over them.

Hence, the key to seeing the real side of someone is to see them tested. The best way is to know how they react under duress.

People will change their principles when under duress - take note of what they say. In times of extreme duress, it is easy for people to adjust the rationale for their behavior.

This obviously might be difficult if you are just meeting someone. There is a huge chance that the person you are meeting might not be under duress. This, however, is a great way to know and read people in the long run.

You cannot really say you know people you think you know when you've only seen them happy. Seeing them under duress will expose their real character.

One of the keys to reading people effectively is the ability to see through this front that most people put up.

Final Thoughts

This is a detailed chapter on reading people, but there is a point you need to hold onto dearly. When all else fails, be sure to listen to your gut. As emphasized at the beginning of this chapter, we are all designed to read people by nature. Your instinct is designed to keep you alive, and you have to trust it!

Chapter 9
Personality Type Explained

Based on Carl G. Jung's theory of psychological types (Jung, 1971), we can characterize people based on their preference of general attitude: Extraverted (E) vs. Introverted (I), their preference based on two functions of perception: Sensing (S) vs. Intuition (N), and their preference also based on two functions of judging (how they come to conclusions): Thinking (T) vs. Feeling (F).

These areas introduced by Jung represent bipolar dimensions in which each pole stands for varying preferences. According to Jung's theory as well, only one of the four above is dominant, which could either be a function of judging or perception.

Isabel Briggs Myers shed more light on Jung's theory. She further analyzed the judging-perceiving relationship as the fourth variation that affects personality type (Briggs Myers, 1980).

Judging (J) vs. Perceiving (P)

The first basis, Extraversion – Introversion, talks about the source of a person's energy. While an introvert derives energy from within, an extravert relies on the external world to recharge.

The second basis, Sensing – Intuition, talks about how a person receives information. A sensing individual absorbs and believes all information received from the outside world. Intuition, on the other hand, is used by a person who relies on their imaginative world to believe information.

The third basis, Thinking – Feeling, talks about how someone processes information. A thinking person will consult logic before making decisions. On the other hand, Feeling means that emotions guide the decisions, in other words, they act based on what they feel.

The fourth basis, Judging – Perceiving, talks about how a person makes use of the information processed. A Judging person will organize their life events and go by their plan. A Perceiving person will likely seek for more alternatives.

The 16 personality types we get are a result of all possible permutations of the four dichotomies above. They represent which of the poles of the four dichotomies dominates an individual, which defines a person. Each personality type gets a 4-letter acronym which represents the combination of preferences.

The various 16 personality types

ESTJ	ISTJ	ENTJ	INTJ
ESTP	ISTP	ENTP	INTP
ESFJ	ISFJ	ENFJ	INFJ
ESFP	ISFP	ENFP	INFP

The first letter of the personality type represents the preference based on general attitude - "E" stands for extraversion and "I" for introversion.

The second letter of the personality type represents the preference based on the sensing-intuition pair: "S" for sensing and "N" for intuition.

The third letter in the acronym represents the preference in the thinking-feeling pair: "T" is for thinking and "F" for feeling.

The last letter in the pair represents the individual's preference in the judging-perceiving pair: "J" for judging and "P" for perception

Explaining the 16 Personality Types

In understanding and analyzing people, an idea of the various personality types is very important.

The Supervisor – ESTJ Personality

Extraverted Sensing Thinking Judging type

You see supervisors at the positions of authority in school, churches, and industries. This is because they are social and community minded. They like to associate with a variety of clubs, institutions, and associations, as they are liberal with their time and energy. Being a leader, they are outspoken and do not find it difficult issuing orders. They are loyal to authority and expect loyalty from subordinates.

They are pretty good at making schedules, plans, and so on. They prefer established methods of doing things rather than experiments. They are firm and expect the same of others. They evaluate other people based on their compliance with schedules and plans.

Supervisors stand out for being industrious. When young, they are hardworking and are outstanding for the respect they show their parents and authority figures. They never miss schedules, homework, are reliable, and honor appointments. They rarely question the teacher's assignments or method of instruction. Even as adults, these values manifest in their personal life and every other area of their lives when they grow up.

Supervisors, being extroverts, have a large circle of friends, with the tendency to maintain friendship for years. They value marriage and parenthood. They attach much meaning to social gatherings, get togethers, ceremonies, reunions, weddings, parties, etc. In social settings, you see them getting along easily with everyone. They could be a bit formal, but they are friendly and warm as well.

Notable supervisors in history are George Washington and Mike Wallace.

The Inspector – ISTJ personality

Introverted Sensing Thinking Judging type

A word that sums up the characteristics of the inspectors is "super-dependable." Wherever they are, they have a high sense of duty, especially when they are responsible for someone or something. They try to uphold rules and standards.

Inspectors can be referred to as the true guardians of institutions. While they are always patient with their job, superiors, and laid down principles, they do not tolerate insubordination. They value people that know what is expected of them and follow the rules. Inspectors will ensure that appointments and schedules are kept, goods are inspected, and everything is as expected. They expect everyone to follow rules.

They are not as talkative as the Supervisor Guardians ESTJs, yet they are very sociable. They are also likely to take part in community services like Boy and Girl Scouts, Sunday School, etc. They value family social ceremonies like weddings and Thanksgiving. They can, however, be shy if the occasion gets rowdy.

They are not the type to value fancy gatherings. Their expressions are plain and down to earth. Their attire is simple, and so is their conversation. You can easily see orderliness and neatness in their home and workspace. They would rather go for standard items compared to fancy models.

Notable inspectors in history are Warren Buffet and Queen Elizabeth II.

Provider – ESFJ Personality

Extraverted Sensing Feeling Judging type

Of all the guardians, the providers are the most sociable. They also bear the responsibility of the welfare of people in their care. They offer a bit more than other personality types, which is a good thing as the Earth and everyone on it needs people that will nurture. They go out of their way to make sure that social functions are a success and the needs of others are met.

They value teamwork and ensure that everyone gets along. They are very meticulous and make wonderful chairpersons in charge of occasions like reunions, fundraisers, charity events, etc. They make fantastic masters of ceremonies and can flow with ease and confidence. They take it upon themselves to relate with people on a personal level and will know everyone by name. They make terrific hosts and makes sure everyone has what they need.

They are friendly and outgoing, like relating with people, and will often strike up conversation with strangers. Providers value friendships and family traditions and they make it a duty to remember birthdays.

Providers are very sensitive to the need of others. In fact, they stand out as being the most sympathetic of all the personality types. As a result of this, they tend to be self conscious and sensitive to what others think of them. Personal criticisms do not go down well with them, even though appreciation makes their world go round.

Notable providers in history are Louis B. Mayer and Dave Thomas.

Protector – ISFJ Personality

Introverted Sensing Feeling Judging type

The primary interest of this group is the safety and security of those they care about – almost everyone in their life. The gene of the protector is made up of loyalty and responsibility, and they derive fulfillment in keeping others from bad things. They are not the type to value speculations, rather, they will flow with principles that have been tried and tested. Because of this, protectors will not find fulfillment if the rules at work are constantly changing.

They love to be of service to others and love to assist the less privileged compared to other personality types. Not as talkative and outgoing as the Provider Guardians [ESFJs], many misinterpret their shyness for coldness when in fact they are sympathetic, warm hearted, and will happily offer themselves to anyone in need.

Protectors are often willing to dedicate long hours to work and wouldn't mind doing jobs that others avoid. They thrive when they work solo. When they lead, they are more likely to do things themselves rather than delegate. They are not the type to give up. They value being thorough and frugal and hardly spend on frivolities.

Being a protector, they tend to prepare for emergency via savings and are ready to help in times of need. They tend to overwork themselves and are also often misjudged. In fact, people take their contributions for granted and they hardly get the gratitude they deserve.

Notable protectors in history are George W. Bush and Mother Teresa.

Promoter – ESTP Personality

Extraverted Sensing Thinking Perceiving type

Promoters are people that make the world lively. They are people of action. In other words, they are people that bring life to places and events. They love new activities and events and have the capacity to even make a routine and boring activity exciting. They are optimistic, bold, daring, and see possibilities in everything. They are the go getters and are undaunted by disasters. They are good at negotiating and make superb entrepreneurs, as they can come up with deals and enterprises in a way that is mysterious to others.

They value the fine and exquisite things like the best food, wine, latest cars, and trending clothes. They tend to know a lot of people and know just the right thing to say to everyone.

They are charming, charismatic, confident, and popular. They have the right stories and jokes to delight their circle of friends. While they value friendship and excitement, they hardly allow anyone to get close to them. They are not so good with commitments and situations where they will have to adhere to a set of rules.

Notable promoters in history are Winston Churchill and Franklin D. Roosevelt.

Crafter – ISTP Personality

Introverted Sensing Thinking Perceiving type

They are distinguished for their dexterity with tools, machines, equipment, and all sorts of instruments. They have the capacity to learn, master, and command tools such that they can learn and be an expert at all sorts of crafts that use tools. Even as infants, they loved playing with objects that are useful.

They love actions and things that give them joy. They love playing with fishing gear, boats, racing cars, scuba gear, hunting rifles, and so on. They love excitement that comes from water skiing, surfing, and racing cars. They play well and hard, often exposing themselves to danger. They are known to be risk takers.

Their form of communication is via their actions, hence they show little interest in developing their language skills. They could be isolated at work or in school, although it is easy for them to spot and play with their kind.

Their loyalty and generosity to friends, families, teammates, and colleagues is second to none. They do not mind sacrificing their time to take part in a community building project, home remodeling and repairs, etc. One of their shortcomings is their insubordination to authority, as rules and regulations are unnecessary restrictions. They value the freedom that comes from their dexterity with tools.

Notable crafters in history are Bruce Lee and Lance Armstrong.

Performer – ESFP Personality

Extraverted Sensing Feeling Perceiving type

They are distinguished by their extraordinary skills in comedy, music, and drama. This explains why they have the ability to delight the people around them with warmth. In whatever they are doing, there is no dull moment with them, as they take interest in lightening up, desisting from worry, and motivating others to do the same.

They are born entertainers and love the attention that comes from entertaining others. They seek the company of others whenever possible, as they are not always comfortable being on their own. They are smooth talkers, always telling jokes and interesting stories. They thrive on making fun of things, no matter how serious. They fancy the best food and latest fashion in cars, drinks, and music.

Their tendency to enjoy life is also their shortcoming, because it makes them more prone to all forms of temptations. They never seem to get enough of pleasure and variety. They will likely jump at anything that promises fun and a good time, without much thought of the consequences.

They are optimistic and always ignore worry and troubles, as they believe all will be well. They are very generous, kind, and stinginess is not in their vocabulary. They are liberal givers and believe in giving what they have to all, hence, they do not believe in saving.

Notable Performers in history are Elizabeth Taylor and Bill Clinton.

Composer – ISFP Personality

Introverted Sensing Feeling Perceiving type

While other Artisans identify with people, tools, and entertainers, Composers have an inborn ability to devote themselves to work with textures, aromas, flavors, tones, and color. They dedicate long and lonely hours into their work. They are not the type that plans or prepares. They like the spur of the moment.

Composers are known for painting, dancing, sculpting, and skating. They do things for the fun of it, with an innate ability to immerse themselves into their activities. They are very kind and sensitive to the pains of others. They get along easily with kids, as if they share a bond of trust.

It is quite difficult to observe the composer, hence misunderstanding them is common. This could be because they express themselves mostly in works of art and not verbally. They are not the type to take an interest in public speaking or chit chat. Rather, they enjoy being in touch with life via the senses. They are interesting personalities nonetheless, but they express themselves better through non verbal communication.

Notable composers in history are Bob Dylan and Steven Spielberg.

Teacher – ENFJ Personality

Extraverted Intuitive Feeling Judging type

Teachers are endowed with the natural ability to lead others – students and trainees. They are capable of reaching out and bringing forth anyone's potential. They are very skilled at coming up with a variety of fascinating activities for their students. Their greatest strength is their ability to believe in all their students and see potential, something hidden to others.

They are notable for giving themselves over to help others. They are warm, outgoing, and expressive. They are good with language and have a high tendency to be charismatic public speakers. Because of their distinct verbal activities, they exert good influence in groups and wherever they are.

They value planning and love a life of organization. They will schedule commitments and obligations well ahead of time and will surely honor them. More than other personality types, they are pretty tolerant of others and easy to get along with.

They are known for their high sense of intuition, with a keen insight into themselves and others. They have their life in order and can read others with some level of accuracy. They show sympathy and identify easily with others, which makes them feel connected to others. With this, they take sincere interest in the joys and sorrows of people.

Notable teachers in history are Oprah Winfrey and Pope John Paul II.

Counselor – INFJ Personality

Introverted Intuitive Feeling Judging type

Counselors have a strong intuitive desire to contribute to the welfare of others. Their fulfillment comes from interacting with others, nurturing potential in them, and guiding them to engage their potential. They enjoy working in solitude, as well as with individuals or groups as long as their 'alone-time' does not suffer. They are great listeners, kind, positive, and see the best in people. They do not make good leaders, but they do a terrific job of making their impact felt behind the scenes.

They form a very small percentage of the entire human race. They do not share their intimate feelings with others except their loved ones. They live a private life and hardly let people in. They value smooth work and thus are a true addition to any team. They cooperate with others and value human systems.

They are blessed with vivid imaginations and are pretty poetic. Their language skills are seen in their manner of communicating with others on a personal level. Being highly intuitive, it is easy for them to recognize other people's emotions.

Notable counselors in history are Eleanor Roosevelt and Sir Alec Guinness.

Champions– ENFP Personality

Extraverted Intuitive Feeling Perceiving type

Champions, just like the other idealist, are pretty rare. They thrive on intense emotional experience. To a champion, life is fun, exciting, and presents good and bad to all. A champion seeks to experience all that life has to offer. They are very outgoing and love to share their experiences with others. They have a strong drive to speak out on issues and events, making them the most inspiring of the personality types.

They value personal authenticity and always strive to be themselves. Their sense of intuition is high, which gives them the ability to easily read people and reveal what is going on with others. With a keen sense of intuition, Champions are capable of noting what other personality types will miss about others. They are always prepared, as if expecting an emergency, and nothing can catch them unawares.

Champions value human relationships, hence they have a wide circle of personal relationship. Their interactions with people are always warm. They are charismatic and easy going. They are spontaneous and dramatic, which makes others enjoy their company.

Notable Champions in history are Charles Dickens and Edith Wharton.

Healer – INFP Personality

Introverted Intuitive Feeling Perceiving type

Healers approach the world with a calm attitude. They could appear shy and distant to others, but personally they are cool and extremely caring, more than any other personality type. They keep their personal circle small and show great care to these few special people. They value healing the conflict that troubles others and restoring the health of their loved ones and community.

To healers, the world is an ethical place loaded with wondrous possibilities and potentials. They have the tendency to make extraordinary sacrifices for people they believe in or a cause they are passionate about. They make up a very little of the population and are extremely private.

Healers welcome new ideas and developments at work. They are patient and seek to understand complex topics. They are, however, not a fan of routine details. They relate well with others, stemming from their keen awareness of people's feelings. Being reserved in nature, they are happy working alone and will follow their heart and not their head when making decisions. They are naturally drawn to scholarly activities, have a flare for language, and are good with interpreting stories.

Notable healers in history are Vincent van Gogh and George Orwell.

Fieldmarshal – ENTJ Personality

Extraverted Intuitive Thinking Judging type

They are known for their ability to lead others, a characteristic that is evident in them from an early age. You will see them taking command in groups and organizations. Most often, they also cannot explain how they got to be leaders. This is, however, not surprising, as they have a strong natural drive to give direction whenever needed in a bid to achieve the overall goal.

They care about the end goal and policy rather than regulations. More than any other personality type, they tend to be able to visualize where the direction of the company or organization is going and communicate this to others. They are known for high coordination and organization skills. With this, they are good at generalizing, systematizing, and showcasing their ideas to others. They perform better at organizing compared to others.

They enjoy being executives and easily rise to position of authority. They devote their entirety to their job and can often get lost in their devotion. In any field, they make good administrators, with the ability to organize their division into a smooth running system. They plan well in advance and consider long and short term goals.

They are motivated only by concrete reasons and they do not bank much on feelings as conviction to do something. They prefer to have their ideas thought and planned out before springing into action. They honor laid down procedures but are quick to dismiss any procedure that is not effective. They have a low tolerance for error as well.

Notable Fieldmarshals in history are Julius Caesar and Margaret Thatcher.

Mastermind – INTJ Personality

Introverted Intuitive Thinking Judging type

Masterminds make the best planners. They are naturally equipped with the ability to manage complex operations that involved many stages. They are good at contingency plans and finding alternatives to seemingly difficult situations. They will hardly set out any project without a clear direction and other backup plans.

They are very rare and do not fancy leadership positions, even though their leadership skills are superb. They will hardly take charge except when others reveal their leadership abilities alongside their pragmatic skills which make them effective leaders. They do not value the restriction that comes from rules and principles. They only flow with ideas that makes sense - others gets dismissed. All of this stems from their affinity for efficiency.

You will often see them take up positions of authority in their career. They can dedicate long hours into their work and goals, and they require others to work the same. They are fascinated by problem solving and will carefully sort out tangled issues. They hardly voice out any negative comments and care more about the accomplishment of the goal, rather than past errors.

They are pretty self confident with a strong self will. They prioritize making decisions and value the gathering of facts to come up with a decision. They will consider all available facts before making a decision or embracing an idea.

Notable masterminds in history are Walt Disney, Isaac Newton, and Dwight D. Eisenhower.

Inventor – ENTP Personality

Extraverted Intuitive Thinking Perceiving type

The ability of inventors to build manifests from a young age which grows with them into adulthood. Society is not blessed with many of them, although they have a great impact on society. With innovation as part of their building blocks, they are always seeking for new and better ways of doing things. In fact, they are the experts at coming up with effective means to accomplish goals. Inventors are the type to challenge the status quo and will hardly succumb to traditional ways of doing things. This makes them bubble with fresh and new ideas at work and on any project.

They are curious and always seek out for diverse ways of solving problems, no matter how complex. They are filled with ideas, but only value ideas that make action possible. They have a large circle of friends and value their initiatives. They are simple, easy going, and hardly critical. They can break down their complicated ideas to others and also follow the ideas of others.

They are not so enthusiastic about routines and prefer to work in an environment that does not constrict them to one. They are good at bringing balance to human relationships, quick to grasp any institutional politics, and have a drive to understand people. You will see them mostly at the forefront of impossible situations, as impossibility is seen as a challenge.

Notable investors in history are Richard Feynman, Thomas Edison, and Benjamin Franklin.

Architect – INTP Personality

Introverted Intuitive Thinking Perceiving type

These are the brains behind all complex theoretical systems like new technology and school curricula, and are not limited to building roads and bridges. Architects see the world as a complex system that needs analysis, understanding, and re-organization. They have a good understanding of fundamental laws and principles which helps their design.

Architects in society are pretty rare. They are distinguished by their great precision in thoughts and speech. No errors, inconsistencies, contradictions, or patterns can escape them. An architect finds it easy to point out errors even in speech or casual conversation. They make terrific debaters, as their skill in constructing pragmatic arguments gives them an edge. They see all discussion as a means to search for knowledge.

They are very patient in listening to others, even so called amateurs, if they have something meaningful to say. They do not fancy celebrities or people that command authority as a result of their office. They value only what gives meaning to them.

They seem difficult to know and could be reserved except with close friends. They find it difficult to let people in. They are good at tasks that require the utmost concentration and love the solitude that comes with working solo. They tend to be carried away by analysis and can shut others off once obsessed with it. They value intelligence and strive to understand the universe. They could be impatient with others who are not capable of following them.

Notable architects in history are Albert Einstein, Adam Smith, and Charles Darwin.

Final Thoughts

This has been a comprehensive chapter on the various personality types. In your relations with people, an idea of the various personality types can give you insight into who they are at their core. This will help in understanding and relating with them easily. You get to know their strengths and weaknesses and not get offended when they act 'unexpectedly.'

Chapter 10
The Power of a Handshake

Apart from your body language, the kind of handshake you give has a lot to say about you. It can make an astounding impact on the people you meet. You might not have reasoned it, but a handshake can invoke someone's emotions. Consider these two scenarios:

A man in his mid 50s entered the board room. He made eye contact with you and extended his arms. With mild force, he grasped your hand and shook it with a warm smile.

He must be a notable figure in the firm, you thought.

In contrast, you encountered another top level employee. You reached out for a handshake and he grasp your fingers for a while. It felt awful, you thought. You feel embarrassed and unwelcomed, even though a part of you seems to disregard it as unintentional.

There is a big chance you do not remember the last handshake you had. You will hardly remember them, since they are pretty normal handshakes. However, I bet horrible ones will linger in your mind. The weak, lifeless handshake and the one with a wet and sweaty palm; I bet you remember many of those.

A handshake is just like other forms of non verbal communication that speaks louder than words. Handshakes have existed for decades and play an important role in social culture. They serve as a form of salutation, bring people together, solidify relationships and create trust.

There is a lot of evidence that points to the fact that people form opinions based on a simple gesture – the handshake.

Why is a Handshake so Important?

Most forms of interaction and conversation begin with a handshake, especially with someone who is not too close to you. Meeting the panel of interviewers, a business meeting, meeting an acquaintance for the first time etc., all involve a handshake.

You create an impression with a handshake, one you will hardly get a second chance at. In just a couple of seconds, it sends volumes of information about you. It expresses your personal characteristics, with a powerful ability to dictate how the interaction proceeds.

With a good handshake, you can seal a deal or land a job, even without knowing it. Besides, even if you are not sure of the kind of impression your handshake gives, I bet you will not want to take the chance of giving a bad handshake.

Believe it or not, there are many forms of handshakes. We have the awkward turtle, the fist bump, the turkey, the lumberjack, and the lobster claw. These are, however, not the types of handshakes you want to form your first impression. This is because your handshake has the capacity to set the tone for the entire meeting, as it forms part of the first impression someone has of you. Many of us have been on the receiving end of a horrible handshake which translates to the fact that we are all giving bad handshakes.

Your handshake is way more than an ordinary initial greeting gesture. It is the first connection with a potential client, candidate, or partner. This is why it is vital to establish and solidify such connections before diving into real interaction. It creates a sense of trust and welcome between parties. Bear in mind that handshakes are two way streets, and both sides of the coin are equally vital.

A study done by management experts at the University of Iowa examined the interaction of candidates in job interviews (Reuters, 2008). One of their discoveries about a handshake was that it is:

"one of the first nonverbal clues we get about the person's overall personality, and that impression is what we remember."

They stated that while people prepare and even go for training in interview questions, dressing, and even their manner of walking, the most significant aspect of all, the handshake, has no training for it whatsoever!

How to Give a Good Handshake

From years of practice, insight, and advice from colleagues, I have some proven and tested tips on giving the perfect handshake. Your handshake does not have to be awkward anymore. Just like the guy in our opening example, you can have an awesome handshake that will carry power and command influence.

- Extend your hand, the right hand. Since it is customary to shake with the right hand, be sure this hand is free before walking into a room. Let your file, briefcase, laptop, notebooks, or writing materials be in your left hand.
- Let your handshake be from thumb to thumb. It should be firm with at most two shakes. Your grip should neither be so hard that the other person will be hurt nor should you be too enthusiastic with it.
- Avoid having cold drinks or bottles of water in your hand. It makes your hand feel cold and clammy, which might be uncomfortable to the other party.
- Let your hands be extended vertically with your thumbs and fingers out. Your palm should not be face down or up, as it signifies being dominant or submissive. Your thumb should be pointing to the ceiling.
- In a formal setting, avoid putting your hands over the handshake.
- A handshake is not complete without eye contact. When you reach out your hands, look the other party in the eye and smile. This combination is powerful and carries a lot of meaning - for instance, that you value their presence and time.

- While shaking hands, your left hand should be free unless you are carrying something. It should not be in your pocket, either.
- It is a good idea to stand for a handshake.
- Make sure your palm is connected web to web with the other person before you shake.
- Shake from the elbow, not the shoulder or wrist, and be sure to match the other person's grip.

All of these tips can be a lot to keep in mind. However, if you do not remember anything else, be sure to combine your handshake with a smile and eye contact. This will give a good impression to the other person and likely make the meeting favor you.

Mastering a confident handshake can be tricky, but it is not necessarily difficult. Bear in mind that you have to practice, as it brings perfection. Start with families and friends - don't wait until you meet the next stranger or client.

As an extra tip, should you by any chance fumble in giving a good handshake, avoid being too hard on yourself. Rather, be sure to tap into some other tactics to take the mind of the other person off the handshake. You could compliment them or ask a question. While you might not get a second chance to make a first impression, you can always make up for it.

Types of Handshakes to Avoid

Handshakes come in various types with quite a few modifications. This part of the chapter will examine briefly the various forms of bad handshakes you should avoid. Do not be fixated on the names, as it might differ from the name you are used to. The idea is to know what these handshakes constitute and the impression they give.

The Bone-Crusher

More than anything, always strive for a firm handshake, as it shows confidence. The point, however, is to not exert too much dominance by overdoing it. Besides portraying you as aggressive, it shows arrogance which might make anyone you are meeting switch to the defensive mode. Also, do not forget that it hurts.

The Limp Noodle

Both extremes of handshakes (too much pressure and an excessively weak handshake) are bad. In this regard, you do not want to appear nonchalant or like you are not giving effort when someone extends a hand to you. The impression this shows is lack of interest in the person or meeting or simply lack of confidence. If your intention is to be gentle with a female colleague, think again. Most female professionals want to be treated the same way as a male colleague.

The Fancy Fool

It is okay to be creative with the handshake by trying new things like the fist bump. You do not, however, want to do this in a formal setting, as this clearly demonstrates immaturity. It is best done among peers, close friends, and family.

The Lingerer

You have given a firm, warm handshake. But you are still holding onto the arm for three seconds or more. This is a clear sign of desperation. The best handshakes span no more than three second. Abide by this - let the hand go before it becomes desperate.

The Look Away

Offering a handshake without eye contact is not complete. In addition to eye contact, be sure to smile. You might be sending the wrong signal if you don't - a sign of insecurity, lack of confidence, or even suspicion.

The Clammy Handshake

In my opinion, this is the worst handshake to receive. It is outright disgusting when you have sweaty hands and you offer such to another person. If you are the type of person whose hands are always sweaty, be sure to offer the other person the courtesy of clean hands and go about with a handkerchief. Offering a clammy hand will not only ruin the other person's mood, but will give a bad impression of you.

Other Tips on Giving a Good Handshake

Be sure, when it is ideal, to initiate a handshake. This could be quite tricky, because initiating a handshake can be seen as being proactive, but in some settings it could be passed off as rude. Make sure you are aware of the cultural setting or the ideal situation before initiating a handshake.

Feel and read the hand. We have emphasized several times that handshakes say so much about a person. This is because handshakes are quite personal as they involve physical contact (touch) with the other person. As a result of this, do not offer a cupped hand or bent fingers. Wrap your fingers around the other person's hand and feel it for the brief moment of the interaction.

The movement of your hands should come from your elbows and not your hands. The grip must be firm with the thumbs locked.

There are times you did not expect a handshake. You are walking down the stairs and you bumped into someone. Suddenly they offered their hands as they approach you and you felt inclined to shake hands, putting them in charge. You can turn the table around offer them a glove handshake (put your other hand over yours and their clasped hands). With this, you have slowed down their momentum, putting yourself in charge.

There are times the direction of your palm should be upward or sideways. Although it is not ideal to offer handshakes while sitting, if you do, offer your hand with the palm facing up. This is a terrific move, especially when you are not so sure of the capacity of the other person. Be careful with this, however, as it is like handing the control of the handshake to the person.

Take note of your overall body language and posture during a handshake. We assume that you are standing while offering the handshake. Be sure to lean in a little with your palm against the other person's. Should the handshake take a little longer than usual, take a step back, as it sends a clue to let them break the grip. If you are seated, be sure to have your back erect while giving the handshake. Avoid bending over or bowing unless you are greeting a person of higher authority.

Avoid patting the other person on the shoulder unless you are in a position to convey care or sympathy - for instance, showing support for a loss - or you are higher in authority like the boss or employer. Be sure to give the person room to shake your hand. Avoid holding the hand for a while and then yanking it away. This is perceived as rude.

Male – Female Issue

In times past, men and women were not supposed to shake hands. But with rise in civilization and the emergence of women in the business world, everyone shakes hands. A man is thus expected to offer the same firm handshake to a woman in a formal setting. In a social situation, however, it is ideal that a woman offers her hand first. In Europe, both in business and social gatherings, the ideal is for a woman to extend her hand first.

In general, the person with the higher status, whatever sex, will extend the hand first. This is peculiar to western culture. In the case that a woman walks up to a man and offers her hand, initiating the handshake, she's sending a message to him and other observers that her status is equal to, if not greater than, his.

Handshakes vary from culture to culture. In Japan, a light handshake and a nod is appropriate, while in the Middle East, they offer a limp and lingering handshake. In visiting other cultures, be sure to do your homework. It takes seconds to build first impressions which last.

Chapter 11
Understand Yourself and Your Behavior: Why Behavior Matters

In understanding one's personal behavior, self awareness or perception matter. If we use the personality and behaviors of the parties involved to ascertain the form of non verbal communication, understanding oneself, as well as our baseline behavior, is crucial.

People, from time to time, do send the wrong or unintended signal. Signals that contradict their intentions result from a lack of understanding of themselves and their behaviors. This chapter will discuss six major keys that can help you understand yourself. These keys are exact reflections of how unique you are as well as your baseline tendencies. It is good to emphasize that the process of understanding the self is a long one.

However, these six keys can guide you in learning a lot of things about yourself.

Your Values

What do you hold dear? What are your values? Your value system is a definition of who you are, as they define all you do and how you go about your actions. Not only that, it reflects greatly in your interaction and relation towards others. Many times, your values are reflected, directly or indirectly, via your non verbal communication approaches.

Your values are what gets your ball rolling. They form the basis of your behavior and personality. A critical analysis of what excites you will give insight into who you are. This could open you up to parts or dimensions of yourself you never knew existed.

Your Strengths and Weaknesses

One of the most generic questions asked during an interview is: "What are your strengths and weaknesses?" The interviewer is not just asking a random question. This question is important, because humans are a combination of strength and weakness. Your strengths are a combination of your talents, inclinations, natural abilities, and patience. They are unique to you, and essential parts of your makeup. Your weaknesses could be impatience, anger...anything you are not proud of, in short.

You will poorly define your abilities and skills without adequate knowledge of your strengths and weaknesses. This explains why employers make sure you supply this information. Your strengths could make you stand out and gain a better result in your career and life as a whole.

Your Temperament

According to the Hippocrates Theory, all humans can be grouped into four main temperament types. A careful examination of these temperament types has led to the acceptance that the basis of human behavior revolves around them. In other words, your temperament determines a lot about many aspects of your life, including your relationships with people and the world as a whole.

In fact, there is a direct link between behavior and temperament. Temperament is seen as a detailed description of people's tendencies and preferences.

Your Life Goals

Where does your interest lie? What do you look forward to becoming in the future? Is there any motivation that guides your path towards your choice? Many people's goal in life has a lot to say about them.

Your actions and experience also matter a lot. What you find important, what makes you tick, exists because there is an attraction between you and such things. In this regard, identifying what makes you tick, what matters to you, and the experiences that shape your life will give you insight into yourself.

Your Interests

In other words, what excites you? What are the things that catch your attention and keep you glued? The behavior and attitude of people towards what interests them differs. For instance, if you have a great interest in animals, I would not be surprised if you chose to work in a zoo or game reserve due to your interest.

Your interests have the capacity to drive you to do something. It stimulates your curiosity, making you focused. They keep the brain firing impulses, and since it is an important part of our makeup, they influence our behaviors and allow us to control them.

Your Biorhythm

Some people are at the best version of themselves just after waking up, so that is when their productivity is higher. Other people feel this way in the evening, hence they perform at their best then. This subtle difference has a lot to say about a person.

A good knowledge of this "biorhythm" can give you insight into your personality and also determine when you function best.

What Your Behavior Says About Your Personality

We go about our daily activities and interactions everyday in a rather spontaneous way. We hardly think about our habits even though they carry a wealth of information about our personality. From the way you brush your teeth to your reaction to the street beggar, they all hold significant information about who you are.

This is because in little behaviors, you get to see critical truths which reveal a person's emotions, values, and their general disposition towards life. Following are a few personal behaviors and what they reveal.

Your Walking Style

A body language expert, Patti Wood, reveals that the way you stroll conveys a telling message about you (Wood, n.d). If you charge ahead by balancing your weight forward, and fix your gaze ahead, you are probably focused and ambitious. However, people might consider this manner of walking cold and unwelcoming. A shy, introverted person, on the other hand, will be lighter on their toes with their eyes downcast.

Also, people who walk and scan the environment with their eyes are socially conscious even though they like to be the center of attention. And lastly, people that walk with their weight on their legs with a smooth gait love being around people and are team oriented.

How You Go About Shopping

Your manner of shopping also carries and reveal loads of information about you. Some people devote a small time to shopping. They already know what they want to buy and where they are going to get it. If they are going to the supermarket, they are likely loyal to a particular brand or chain. These kinds of people are focused, goal centered, and key planners.

Some people, alternatively, head to the market or mall without a distinct goal of what they want. They would rather tour the length and breadth of the mall looking for anything that piques their interest. This is a clear reflection of impulsiveness and lack of organization.

Finally, some people will scrutinize each product, checking the fat and sugar content, details, and the expiry date before selecting a product. These are the perfectionist who pay attention to details.

Your Email Style

Your email style can also give up a couple of things about your persona. For instance, a well structured email without grammar or typing errors points to a perfectionist, and a conscientious person.

Lengthy mails could indicate a needy personality and a tendency to be thorough. While introverts will skip the chit chat and get down to business, an extrovert will likely be a little casual and free with their choice of words.

Punctuality

Your attitude towards time also has a lot to say about you. Some people are fond of always being late and will have formulated the perfect excuse. The impression this gives is undependability. You are slow and relaxed in your approach to things and love to enjoy every moment. The other category of people value time and will hardly miss appointments even by a minute. These types of people value time and could be seen as quite neurotic.

Lastly, people that arrive on the dot can be said to have traits of dependability and agreeableness.

How You Eat

A Los Angeles based behavioral expert, Juliet Boghossian, reveals that there is a direct link between eating habits and personality traits (Boghossian, n.d.). According to Boghossian:

"Food-related habits can, in fact, reveal facets of an individual's personality and behavioral tendencies."

As a result, slow eaters, Boghossian added, like to be in charge and are keen on appreciating and enjoying life. They can be said to be confident and level-headed. People who devour their meal could be said to be ambitious, firm, focused, and goal oriented. Boghossian added that,

"The speed at which you eat reveals the speed at which you take on and enjoy life,"

Picky eaters did not grow out of the habit of likes and dislikes they had in their childhood days. And finally, people who are not keen on trying new food are linked to characteristics like sensation seeking and anxiety.

Your Handwriting Style

Graphology teaches the patterns and the physical characteristics of various people's handwriting. The analysis of the pattern of writing can point to some personality traits and characteristics in a person. Graphologists, people skilled at analyzing handwriting, reveal that a person's handwriting can reveal as many as 5,000 traits (Gal, 2018). A few of these are:

- **How do you dot your "i's"**: If the dot for your I is high up the page, handwriting experts reveals that you have an active imagination. On the other hand, a closely dotted 'I' reveals a person that is detailed and organized. If you dot your I with a circle, you are still in touch with your childhood, with the tendency to be playful. There is a big chance you are a procrastinator if you dot your I to the left.

- **How legible your signature is**: The way you sign your documents also matters. You are highly confident and comfortable with yourself if your signature is legible. A private or really conscientious person will put forward an illegible signature.
- **How you cross your "t's"**: Handwriting experts also reveal that the way you cross your "t's" could reveal some information about you. If you cross your "t's" with a long cross, you are a determined, strong headed, and energetic person. If you use a short cross on the other hand, you might be considered as lazy. What about your lowercase t's? If you cross them high up, there is a big chance you have lots of goals and targets. If you cross it low, this means you do not have many challenging goals.
- **What do your "y" hooks look like**: The way your lowercase "y" is looped also reveals a couple of things about you. If you have a broad loop, you probably have a lot of friends. A slender loop, on the other hand, means you keep your circle close and are selective of those you let in. A long hook also means you love adventure while a short hook could signify that you are the home-body type.
- **How you loop your lowercase "l"** (cursive): If your 'l' is widely looped, you are probably a relaxed person. A narrow l, on the other hand, could signal a careful person.
- **Size of word and letters:** Large letters indicate that you crave attention and want to be understood. This could reveal an extroverted personality. Small letters, on the

other hand, reveal focus and concentration and might be associated with an introverted personality.

- **Slant:** If writing tends to slant towards the right, it could indicate a sentimental and slightly impulsive person. If your writing is straight, it could mean you are a logical person. Leftward slant refers to people who love working with things.
- **Pressure:** Excessive pressure could mean someone with strong emotions. Light pressure indicates a simple person with a playful attitude who fancies adventure.
- **Linking of letters:** If your letters are connected, you are a methodological, logical, and careful person. If your letters are spaced, it could indicate an intelligent and intuitive person.

How Your Organize Your Personal Space

By personal space, we mean your closet, bedroom, office desk, inbox, and even your desktop. A person who ensures orderliness in all their personal spaces, making sure their closet, mobile phone, wardrobe, etc. follow a given level of orderliness, reveals a lot about their personality. This likely indicates an orderly person. They prefer stable and tested means of doing something rather than exploring.

On the other hand, they may have a domineering personality if they frown upon anyone or anything that upsets the balance of their space.

Final Thoughts

This chapter has shed light on ways to understand yourself and how you can gain insight into who you are through your personality. The idea is to use these behaviors as a basis, not only to understand ourselves, but other people as well. It is when you can understand what each pattern of behavior stands for that it will be easier to analyze other people well.

All in all, an accurate analysis of a person starts with an inherent ability to accurately understand yourself.

Chapter 12
How to Build Rapport Fast

We all live around people and need people to survive and thrive. This calls for a need to be able to connect with others. In connecting with others, we get to know and access people that share the same interest as us. The inability to connect with people on a deeper level could make you miss out on a wealth of information and resources that could be helpful to you. This is why this chapter will explore how you can develop a soul-like connection with people on all levels, which could help in business, casual, or even romantic relationships.

Rapport can be said to be a close and friendly relationship with people or in a group in which members feel connected and understand one another. It is the kind of relationship that thrives on mutual trust, respect, and an understanding of the concerns of others. Building a strong rapport is vital to improve your chances of having a solid bond between friends, colleagues, partners, clients, lovers, and customers.

Not only will you be able to build rapport with people you already know, if you follow the teachings of this chapter, you can build trust with people that hardly know you. There will be mutual respect between you, and you will regard one another in a better light. This chapter is all about taking the relationship you have with friends and loved ones to another level.

This chapter will be structured into two sections: the first part is the skills and techniques you need to improve rapport building. The next part will discuss the tips that will make this a reality. Let us get started.

Important Skills to Build Rapport Fast

There are times you will meet people and you will feel at home with them almost immediately. You cannot explain it, but you know you've just connected with them instantly. The reason for this is not far fetched: there are parts of them that reflect something about you. They could demonstrate subtle sign of mirroring your posture, sitting positions, gestures, phrases you use, tone of your voice, etc. It's little wonder you felt a connection with them you just could not explain. However, this person was employing the process of mirroring your speech patterns and body language. These are the two major techniques you need to establish rapport with anyone.

Do you want someone to feel free to be themselves with you? Then tapping into the art of mirroring their speech and body language is all you need. This will automatically create trust and a comfortable environment for the other person, be it a stranger or an acquaintance. With these concepts, you can get people to loosen up, open up, be free, and be themselves.

This is not only powerful, but an efficient ways to influence and build rapport with people. The reason is simple - the message they convey builds understanding and trust. Hence, it is not surprising you felt comfortable around them.

This is the basis of how to build rapport. You can use this to your advantage to get your employee to feel at home or gain the trust of someone you like. It is, however, important not to be too obvious, as it could backfire!

In mastering the art of building rapport, follow these steps:

Feel the Connection

In establishing rapport, one of the primary steps is to feel the connection. This connection is a two way thing, because there is a huge chance they are not feeling it if you are not feeling it as well.

Here, the idea is to make the person the center of attention. Make them feel important and relevant. Be sure to have a direct line of view with the person. If possible, stand in front of them and be physically present with them. Give body signals to show you are with them. Look them in the eye while talking, but don't make this too creepy, and nod to show you are paying attention.

Mimic the Pace

In building rapport, we have talked about mirroring body language. Not only body language, however, but the pattern of talking as well. In other words, trying to talk like the other person can make the connection stronger as well.

What is the pattern of speech of the person? Do they talk slowly, fast, or calmly? Gradually copy them. This works best when you both have the same accent. It is effective and not as obvious as mirroring body language, but equally powerful.

What is their Punctuator?

Everyone has something known as a punctuator that they use to express themselves. This usually comes in the form of a body movement like a hand gesture, nodding of the head, and raising of the eyebrows. You, however, need to pay rapt attention to someone to decode their favorite punctuator.

There is a big chance you will make an instant connection with someone if you can identify their punctuator and employ it to let them know you agree with them. For instance, a person that grins to drive home their point will easily connect with you if you also grin and make a statement like, "I see your point."

One of the things about punctuators is that you do not need to utter a word before using it, though this depends on the person you are with.

Why is Rapport So Important?

Building rapport is important if we are to succeed in our personal and professional lives. In hiring an employee, as well, employers will likely favor someone that can easily connect and get on board with the staff. Rapport brings closer connection and understanding between the parties involved, irrespective of the relationship.

Why do you think people make small talk? It is to build rapport with those we are meeting for the first time. This is a tested and universal way of searching for and establishing a common ground with the other party. This bond is vital, as humans tend to be a magnet to others like them.

When you find someone who has a lot in common with you and who shares your ideas and interests, you will more than likely want to be around that person. The reason is because rapport comes easily in such cases.

There are common interests and shared ground. As a result, the interaction and communication goes smoothly and conversation comes with ease.

There are, however, times when no matter how lovely a person seems to be, we just can't seem to get along with them. This is as a result of the absence of a common shared point from which the relationship can thrive. However, all hope is not lost, and you can build rapport. This is what this part of the chapter aims to teach you.

Step by Step Tips in Building Rapport

Break the Ice

This could be the hardest part for most people, especially when with a stranger. I understand that it could be a stressful endeavor starting a conversation with a person you know nothing about. Words may fail you and your throat may be dry.

This is, however, the foundation of successful interaction, especially when interacting with a person you know nothing about. You might feel stressed or nervous, which is normal. However, trying to relax will help. You can practice deep breathing to relax your muscles. With reduced tension, it will be easier to communicate and build rapport.

If your aim is to build rapport with someone you are meeting for the first time, try any or some of the following methods to help both of you communicate effectively. Some of these are:

Use neutral topics for small talk. Your discussion could revolve around the weather, places you have traveled to, etc. This is not the point to start blowing your trumpet and making the conversation personal. You do not want to ask too many direct questions at this stage, either.

In your discussion, look for shared experiences. This will only come when you listen attentively to what the other person is saying. With this, you can find common ground from where you will hit things off.

Subtly try and introduce an element of humor. When you laugh together, you will create harmony. If you are not the funny type, make jokes about yourself or a past awkward situation you were in.

For the entire period of interaction, take note of your body language and other non verbal signals you might be sending. Be sure to maintain eye contact, but do not stare. If you are seated, relax and lean toward the other person. It gives the impression that you are listening closely.

Demonstrate empathy. In other words, let the person know you are on the same page as them. Let them know you see things from their angle. Rapport, as we have been saying, is about establishing similarities and being on the same page. Being empathetic is one of the ways to achieve this.

Communicate, don't interrogate, with the person you are meeting. Their feeling at ease is central to achieving your aim – building rapport. Your manner of communication has a lot to do/say about this.

How Non-Verbal Communication Helps Build Rapport

The purpose of the initial small talk is to build a connection and relax. However, unknown to many people, we build rapport without words and through non verbal channels of communication.

Rapport, as discussed above, comes with matched non verbal signals which include mimicking body movements, eye signals, facial expressions, and the voice pattern.

Rapport comes with instinct, as it is our natural defense against conflicts that people go to lengths to avoid.

The right body language is very vital in building rapport. This is why reading and believing someone's body language comes naturally to us and seems more convincing than what comes out of the mouth. Let us assume you asked a stranger for a bottle of water. He frowns and hands the bottle of water to you. I bet you will be hesitant to collect the bottle of water because his facial expression shows clear disagreement with you. This explains why people will likely go with the body language if what is communicated with the mouth differs from what the signs coming from the body language say. This is why you have to display the right body language to build rapport. In other words, you have to be welcoming, relaxed, and open.

Besides being attentive to what is being discussed, you also have to be sure your communication is on the same page. You can repeat what has been said. This is a useful tactic to give the impression that you are keenly following on the communication. Besides that, you also get to repeat the words of the other person, bringing about similarity and providing the grounds for building rapport.

The manner of talking is equally important in building rapport. A tense or nervous person will talk fast, which could give the impression of being stressed. Based on what we are saying, or the gravity of the communication, we can vary our volume and pitch to sound interesting. This can also affect the person we are communicating with. One tip to put in mind is that talking slowly and softly can help you develop rapport quickly.

Behaviors to Help Build Rapport

In addition to non verbal clues and body language, there are other behaviors you can adopt to build rapport.

If you are both seated, for instance, we recommend that you lean toward the other party. Make sure your hands and legs are uncrossed. This is sending a signal that you are open, which will help both of you communicate freely.

During the period of the discussion, make sure you maintain eye contact for about 60% of the time. Be careful not to make the other party uncomfortable.

While listening, allow the person to talk by making encouraging sounds and gestures.

When you first start talking, use the other person's name. It is polite and helps you to not forget it. Besides, this creates a sort of connection between you two.

Be sure to ask open question, not a yes or no question. This sort of question will keep the conversation flowing.

Employ feedback to summarize and clarify on what the person said.

When you agree with the other person, let the person know, along with the reason. Also, try and build on the person's idea.

Avoid judging the other person before they've had their say. Also avoid any preconceived ideas or stereotypes you might have of the person.

When you make a mistake, admit it. This is a simple and effortless way to build trust fast.

Avoid criticism, give compliments, and be nice.

Above all, smile!

Final thoughts

Building rapport that will last a long time is indeed very easy. You just need to know how to go about it. It is a simple task that you can master and something you most certainly can do. There are people around you blessed with abundant resources. You can develop the needed skills and tactics and tap into these resources from people around you. You can make strong connections with people that will help your course.

It is important to note that building rapport is different from taking advantage of people. This is about developing a strong social circle with the techniques discussed to have stronger and better relationship.

Chapter 13
Mistakes to Avoid When Reading Body Language

We have provided extensive clues on how to read body language. We have also examined various ways in which you will be better off with the ability to read non verbal signals. However, it is good to have some tips up your sleeve to guide you. This is because you might not really experience these advantages if you do not look out for these common mistakes.

By nature, humans are programmed to draw conclusions and inferences on people we meet based on facial and behavioral cues. However, the ability to interpret those gestures in the context of the prevailing situation is essential. This will prevent you from drawing the wrong conclusion about the intention of a gesture.

As a higher species, this nature is inherent in us. Over the years, the ability to make friends and influence others has helped us avoid confrontation.

In whatever setting you find yourself, your ability to read nonverbal signals matters a lot. However, be sure to keep these mistakes in mind, as they can undermine your success.

Ignoring the Context

To have a real interpretation of non verbal cues, the setting is very important. Take in these two scenes for a better explanation:

You come in from work and you notice your daughter at the dining table. She is seated with her head on the table, eyes closed, and shivering.

Consider another scene:

It is a cold winter morning and you see this same girl, seated on your front porch. The north wind is cold and there is a light snowfall.

A careful consideration of these two scenes reveals that the non verbal communication signal is the same. The first scene is obviously a body signal expressing distress, while the other is an expression of someone feeling cold.

Hence, nonverbal communication is best interpreted in relation to the context. To correctly read and analyze someone, be sure to consider the circumstances that influenced their behavior.

Looking for Meaning in a Single Gesture

The best way to interpret nonverbal cues is via what is called gesture cues. In other words, how do the posture, eye cues, movement, and actions translate to a certain point? If you have a single gesture, it could have more than one meaning, or might not even mean anything. However, interpreting that one meaning in relation to other nonverbal cues makes the idea become clearer.

For instance, a lady with crossed legs could be that way for many reasons. It could be in a bid to sit properly, like a lady. However, crossed legs accompanied by a head shake or head tilted backwards will give you a complete picture. With this, you can confidently pass the body language off as being closed or resistant to you.

Excessive Focus on What is Said

Fixating only on what is being said will make you miss the main point and their real intention. And as a matter of fact, the body language will usually reveal the true intention, as it hardly ever lies. Hence, when the body language contradicts what they are saying, be sure to pay attention to the body language.

Imagine this scenario as well, to drive home this point:

A professor was trying to explain to his students why they should do more assignments and field work. He appeared calm and reasonable as he stated his points. However, on reading the list, his body language gave him out. While his reasons portrayed the intention of empowering his student, he shuddered, which was a clear indication that he meant: "You are mature enough to figure this out on your own, I do not want to have to tell you this."

Failure to Understand the Person's Baseline

The idea of a person's behavior under normal circumstances is vital for you to be able to spot deviations.

Here is the kind of thing you should expect without an adequate knowledge of a person's baseline:

I went for a job interview some years back. It was the final of the series of interviews and I had to meet with the CEO. He asked me to walk him through my experiences over the years, which I did, but I knew it was not going well.

Our meeting lasted for almost 45 minutes, and the whole time, this CEO stared at me with an expressionless face. His arms were tightly folded as he listened to me blab about all I had done over the years. There was neither a nod nor any word of affirmation. I managed to finish, and he left the room with a thank you - I knew I flopped.

I was pretty confident that all the vibes I got from his body cues said that I was not the right candidate. You can imagine my shock when, as I managed to get out of the office building, the CEO's assistant walked up to me and told me that the CEO was impressed with my experiences.

In disbelief, my jaw dropped and asked why he would present such a cold reaction if he was impressed. The assistant smiled and said many people have reacted this way, and the CEO would have walked out in the middle of the meeting had I not impress him.

Since I had accepted these nonverbal cues as negative, it affected me, as they were the only ones that the CEO gave. However, for this man, this was his own normal baseline behavior.

Using One's Cultural Bias to Judge Body language

Culture is a set of shared beliefs and values peculiar to a specific group of people. A child learns culture at an early age, although, they could learn it subconsciously via watching others. These values and beliefs are critical to the group's behavior, way of doing things, and, more importantly, how they judge others.

Based on the particular culture, some nonverbal behaviors might be normal and right, while to a stranger, they might be totally off. In other words, what is proper, acceptable, and correct in a culture might not, in fact, be offensive in another culture.

In some African cultures, for instance, it is rude for a child or someone young to look an elderly person straight in the eye when talking. This is a sign of respect common to that culture. Yet, it could be interpreted as weakness or timidity in other cultures.

Final Thoughts

It is an established fact that body language cues cannot be denied. However, you have to be careful in decoding them correctly. Hence, to get the right message body language is conveying, you have to get the idea in relation to the context, consider them in clusters, judge them based on what the person says, know if it is peculiar to the person, and examine the culture.

These five tips will help you get the best out of non verbal communication and use it to your advantage in whatever setting you are!

Chapter 14
How to Make a Fantastic First Impression

According to a 2006 study in Psychological Science, it takes the brain one-tenth of a second upon seeing someone for the first time to process information based on the person's face (Wargo, 2006). This leads to conclusions on the qualities of the person which could revolve around friendliness, competency, honesty, morality, and trustworthiness.

This was as a result of times past when our forefathers encountered strangers and had a split second to determine if the fellow was a foe or an ally. This was critical to the survival of our ancestors.

If you think you have even up to a minute to make a first impression, you might have to reconsider that mindset.

With the above in mind, whatever the course of the meeting, whether it's in business, casual, or a date, you have to have the right tips up your sleeve to make the right first impression. This is why this chapter will examine simple tips that anyone can employ to build a good first impression and have a strong reputation.

Smile

The power of the face is critical in making a good first impression. Your contact will likely read your face first before sizing you up. This is why you have to brand yourself with positivity and friendliness to score points with the other person.

Smiling is very important for many reasons. In fact, after any meeting you have, a smile is one of the things that will linger in your memory even after the meeting.

Bear in mind that this is not about putting a fake grin on your face, as it could pass you off as being inauthentic. Excessive smiling, for instance, could mean an effort to cover up nervousness. This might send the wrong message of being arrogant. A little grinning will go a long way.

You can get others to feel at ease with you and also reduce stress hormones. This has been affirmed by many studies that show smiling improves longevity (Jaffe, 2010). Smiling will also work to help decrease the nervousness brought by meeting a new person for the first time.

Employ the Power of the Handshake

We have dedicated a special chapter to explore the power of handshakes. We have examined how giving the right handshake conveys confidence and can set the tune for a positive interaction.

As we have explained, be sure to employ the tips on giving the right handshakes. Take note of the kinds of handshakes to avoid and be sure to look the other party in the eye when giving the handshake.

Introduction

You want the first couple of seconds with the person you are meeting to be very productive. This is where you have to put adequate thought into your verbal introduction.

You can break the tension with something as simple and basic as "Great to meet you!" If you are the type that does not remember names easily, you can use the intro to reinforce the person's name.

It does not have to be overly involved. For instance, when the person says: "Hi, I'm Jane," with a smile you can say, "Great to meet you, I'm Jake." This is better than replying: "Hello I'm Jake."

Adjust Your Attitude

There is a chance you are having a good day. This will make you happy and you carry a positive aura around you. You could be having a bad day, on the other hand, in which case you will not be as approachable.

As we go about our daily activities, we tend to scan the world and environment around us for threats. This makes us notice and mark out anyone frowning as a potential threat and territory to avoid.

Do not see an attitude as good or bad - rather, think about it in terms of usefulness. A useful attitude is charismatic, welcoming, and full of life, while a useless one is boring, cold, and lifeless. It falls on you to create the sort of attitude that will not mark you as a threat to people. This is a factor of your body language, facial expression, countenance, etc.

If you are nervous, take some deep breaths and remember something that made you laugh really hard. This should be able to calm your nerves enough to make you approachable.

Search for Common Ground

The faster you can find common ground with someone, the better and easier you will be able to establish a connection. Is the person wearing a piece of designer clothing you admire? Does the person have an accent?

This is the simplest way to find common ground, as humans are wired to be drawn to people that are quite similar.

Let the Focus be on the Other Person

In assessing threat when meeting people and getting into new territories, we tend to pay more attention to how we feel rather than the feelings of the other person. Experts, however, advise that it pays off to pay attention to people around you, because humans will always remember how you made them feel.

Speak Clearly

You might have interesting things to say, but without confidence, you won't be able to get your message out. This will, however, make people overlook you, robbing you of the chance to put your best foot forward.

Speak clear, talk slowly, and don't be too loud. You want a calm environment where people can be free around you.

Make Eye Contact

When you make eye contact, the message you are passing across is confidence and an interest in the party you are meeting.

In the Western countries like the United States, for instance, looking someone in the eye is essential to communicate respect. Besides, it also sends the message of interest in the conversation to the other party. Looking around excessively passes on the message of being distracted.

However, you should not look the person in the eye so much that they feel uncomfortable. Break eye contact and make it again.

Employ the Right Body Language

An interesting fact about body language is that many people will mirror other people's body language by instinct.

Have you ever yawned because you saw someone yawn or even heard it? The same way, a smile between a group of people is contagious. Science has it that there is a neuron in the part of the brain which is associated with recognizing faces and reading facial clues (Wikipedia, 2019). It also triggers the mirroring reaction in humans.

It is the mirroring action that makes the other person smile when they see you smile. One thing about mirroring is that it goes both ways. If you can pick and mirror the body language of the person you are with, there is a message that it passes across to them as well – that you feel what they feel.

According to research, if you experience the same emotions, there is a tendency to build trust, connection, rapport, and understanding. This will definitely make a good impression on the person you are with.

Final Thoughts

First impression matters a lot and set the tone for the entire relationship. However, you can get the odds in your favor by mastering simple and un-diabolical ways to get people to like you. The teachings in here will help you know how to put your best foot forward, therefore ensuring every interaction you have is positive and fruitful.

Chapter 15
Dealing With Objections

In the final chapter on learning how to analyze people, I will be shedding light on helpful tips to know if you will be accepted or rejected. This chapter is particularly useful to salesman or people in business trying to close deals. You can decode someone's body language and learn if they will accept or reject your offer by learning how to read the rejection body language.

In every interaction, meeting, or discussion with people, it is not only about what you or the other person says. The success of the interaction hinges on your ability to listen to what your audience is not saying. In other words, you employ your eyes to also "hear" what the various parts of their body are saying.

Learn the Signs of Objections

As we have indicated many times in this manual, do not be so fixated on what a person says. As a matter of fact, the speech and body language could mean different things. However, the cues from the body are usually unconscious, hence it gives people out.

Here are various examples that you will see from various parts of the body that signify objection. Be sure to pay attention to them and use your knowledge to address them accurately before your audience raises their objection. They will think you are actually reading their mind.

Hands and Arms

More than you realize, the hands can reveal a lot - much more than what someone says during conversation. This could relate with the position of the hands or the movements themselves. In whatever interaction you find yourself, be sure to take note of the hand and arm signals that reveal objection. With your knowledge, you can take proactive step to address whatever you feel the objection is.

- When the person you are interacting with plays with an object like a pen, it is a clear indication of boredom. They could also be annoyed. The best tactic to employ in this situation is to give them a chance to be part of the conversation. Ask clarifying questions that will get them to open up about their feelings.
- When the other person is drumming their fingers, it is a clear sign of impatience. This happens when you submit excessive details. This is a clue to cut the chase and quit beating about the bush.
- Hands crossed is an indication that they are not interested in what you are presenting.

- The body or hands turned away show a dislike of the conversation. Bring up another subject or end the engagement. You not only save time, but energy.
- Pointing at you is a sign of intimidation. Ask if they will share their thoughts and calmly clarify any objections they might have.
- A person resting on the armrest or leaning on one arm is bored and wants to leave. You can tackle this by allowing the person to share their views. Be careful, however, because this body language cue is not always accurate. Hence, as discussed in a previous chapter, consider clusters and do not draw conclusions based on a single sign.

Feet and Legs

- If the hands and face prove difficult to read, consider their feet. Even if people want to fake the subtle signals coming from their body, it is hard to do for the feet and legs. Hence, in any interaction, if the person agrees with you, the feet will bear witness.
- A person wiggling their feet or legs is bored. This happens when you have talked too excessively. It might be time to bring them into the conversation.
- If a person you are trying to sell to is tapping their feet, they are likely feeling like they have gained the upper hand. It could also be that they already have an advantage in the negotiation. While this does not necessarily reveal objections, it is a clue that you are not on the winning side.

Eyes

In addition to the feet, the pupils are one of the few body parts that we cannot manipulate. The eyes will clearly reveal or give out anyone that is with or against you. Here are some cues you should watch out for in the eyes:

- Watch the person's pupil for narrowing, as it signifies a serious concern or objection. This is the point where you should slow down and clarify your last point. Better still, you could ask if they have any concerns they would like you to clarify.
- A person staring you down obviously has some concerns or issues about what you are presenting. If you are trying to close a deal or sell a product, take a pause and ask for questions about what you are presenting.
- A person that keeps glancing at the door while you are making a presentation or trying to close a deal is obviously fed up and wants to leave. If you still have some things to say, use this cue and bring them in the conversation. If you are done with your presentation, there is no point keeping them waiting.

Others

Keep an eye out for the following:

- Pursing of the lips reveals a person who has some concerns about you but chooses to keep them private out of courtesy. But these people will surely not agree with you, even though they do not want to hurt your feelings. When you notice this body language, give them a chance to voice their opinions. Even if they are not forthcoming at first, a little persuasion will do.

- People often show a little disagreement with a crinkle of the nose. One thing about this objection sign is that the person is not sure if they are right or wrong. This objection is not fully formed, hence what you feed the person via information will determine if it will be voiced out or addressed. As usual, be sure to ask them to voice their concerns and see if you can address them, even if they feel it is trivial.
- Unconscious scratching of the neck or tension in the neck is a sign of serious doubt. If you notice this from someone you are communicating with, ask if they feel what you said is in line or out of order. With this, you can get your facts right.

Final Thoughts

With these ideas, you know if a potential mate, client, employee, boss, or prospect will object to your proposal. As we have emphasized in this chapter, be sure to pay attention to the cues of objection and address them accordingly. With this, you get better at building relationships, closing deals, and avoid wasting unnecessary time when the signs are clear that your effort is not yielding anything tangible.

Conclusion

If you have been diligent and read this far, you will mostly likely agree that analyzing people is a broad field. There is a wealth of information about the people we meet every day. It is the skill of analyzing people correctly that will help you gain meaningful information on them and interact meaningfully with others. These skills, however, do not come on a platter of gold. The skills will not do you any tangible good if they end up as ordinary knowledge and aren't put into practice.

Analyzing someone can be a lot to take in. You, however, do not have to be an undercover agent to master the art of reading people. This book has broken down all you need to know into a step by step process. It is now time to take what you have learned and put it into action. You can analyze people and determine their real intention, even if their body language is saying another thing. You will also be able to see beyond the veil many people put up, and you get to see people for who they really are.

It is important that I emphasize at this juncture that you approach people you meet on neutral ground. For you to accurately read people, you need to let go of prejudice and bias. Not everyone you meet has an ulterior motive or is out to get you.

Humans are complex creatures. It takes practice and efficiency to see past the veil and attitudes many people put up in daily interactions. The fact is, our subconscious self is constantly giving out information and clues that only the few knowledgeable about human psychology can pick up. Now, you do not have to freak out because of the term "human psychology." Part of the objective at the intro of this book was to break down the psychology of human such that a fifth grader would know how to read people.

If you can dedicate time and practice to the teachings of this manual, you will come out as a superhuman. You get to analyze people correctly, as no body language clue will elude you again. With this, you can now exert your influence on people in a manner that benefits you all.

In everyday interaction with other people, many people do not give themselves over to the idea of getting the best out of the relationship and knowing the other party fully. This is not surprising, as they lack the right skills which will help them relate with others well. However, this book has explained how to make a good first impression, build rapport, and make anyone feel comfortable with you.

All you have to do is dedicate a couple of weeks to diligently practice the teachings of this manual. With time, you will notice tangible improvement in your business, relationships, and all your interactions. It would be a waste of time to read this book without putting the ideas into practice. These skills could take a while to master, so form the habit of refreshing your memory until the art of analyzing people becomes part and parcel to you. I am sure you can tweak the teachings of this manual to any situation you are, even if we did not mention your case exactly.

Hardly will you see an undercover agent announcing to the world that they're an agent. The point here is that you have to be discreet. People can be fiercely protective of their privacy. Besides, people might feel violated if they discover you are trying to analyze them. The worst part is that making it obvious that you are reading people might not get you any tangible results.

All in all, this is your ticket to a positive change and improvement in your life, business, career, and relationships.

Be excited at the world of possibilities that's about to open for you.

References

1. Boghossian J (n.d) "Over 20 years ago, I discovered an incredible correlation between the way people eat and what that revealed about their personalities. Retrieved from https://www.food-ology.com/overview

2. Briggs Myers, I. (1980, 1995) Gifts Differing: Understanding Personality Type

3. Cain A (2017) 11 signs someone might be lying to you. Retrieved from https://www.businessinsider.com/11-signs-someone-is-lying-2014-4

4. Centeno A (n.d). 3 Scientific Tips To Detect Lying | How To Spot Lies Using Body Language. Retrieved from https://www.realmenrealstyle.com/lie-detection/

5. Changing Mind (n.d) Eyes Body language. Retrieved from https://www.changingminds.org/techniques/body/parts_body_language/eyes_body_language.htm

6. Cherry K, (2019). Understanding Body Language and Facial Expressions. Retrieved from https://www.verywellmind.com/understand-body-language-and-facial-expressions-4147228

7. Fadah S (2018) Signs Of Attraction: How Do I Know If They Like Me? Retrieved from https://www.betterhelp.com/advice/attraction/signs-of-attraction-how-do-i-know-if-they-like-me/

8. Gal S, (2018) What your handwriting says about you. Retrieved from https://www.businessinsider.com/what-your-handwriting-says-about-you-2014-7?IR=T

9. Goldman J (2016). 6 ways successful people make a great first impression. Retrieved from https://www.businessinsider.com/6-ways-successful-people-make-a-great-first-impression-2016-9

10. Goman K (2018). Reading body language at work: 5 mistakes you don't want to make. Retrieved from https://www.theladders.com/career-advice/reading-body-language-at-work-five-mistakes-you-dont-want-to-make

11. Impact Factory.(n.d) Influencing Skills - How To Influence People. Retrieved from https://www.impactfactory.com/library/influencing-skills-how-influence-people

12. Jaffe E. (2010) The Psychological Study of Smiling. Retrieved from https://www.psychologicalscience.org/observer/the-psychological-study-of-smiling

13. Jung, C. G. (1971). Psychological types (Collected works of C. G. Jung, volume 6, Chapter X)

14. Lattimer C (n.d) 7 Simple Ways To Be a Positive Influence As A Leader. Retrieved from https://www.trainingzone.co.uk/community/blogs/christinapd/7-simple-ways-to-be-a-positive-influence-as-a-leader

15. Mar, D. (2018) The Power of a Good Handshake A handshake forms the first impression. And you will never get a second chance. Retrieved from https://goodmenproject.com/featured-content/the-power-of-a-good-handshake/

16. Mindvalley (2018) Come Hither: The Body Language Of Attraction And Love. Retrieved from https://blog.mindvalley.com/body-language-attraction/

17. Napier P (2019) The Power of the Perfect Handshake. Retrieved from https://etiquette-ny.com/the-power-of-the-perfect-handshake/

18. Patti Wood (2007) From Patti Wood's book, "The Conflict Cure" Retrieved from https://www.pattiwood.net/article.asp?PageID=10859

19. Pursey K. (n.d) 6 Signs of Insecurity Which Show That You Don't Know Who You Are. Retrieved from https://www.learning-mind.com/signs-of-insecurity/

20. Patti Wood (2007). Recognizing DISC Personalities through Body Language. Retrieved from http://www.pattiwood.net/article.asp?PageID=10859

21. Power of Positivity (n.d) Researchers Explain What Your Habits Say about Your Personality. Retrieved from https://www.powerofpositivity.com/habits-reveal-personality/

22. Reuters (2008) Firm handshakes help grab jobs – study. Retrieved from https://www.reuters.com/article/idINIndia-33471820080508

23. Science of People (n.d) How to Read People Through Their Eye Movements and Uncover Hidden Emotions. Retrieved from https://www.scienceofpeople.com/read-people-eyes/

24. Skills you Need (n.d) Building Rapport. Retrieved from https://www.skillsyouneed.com/ips/rapport.html

25. Stefano R (2018) Why Your Handshake Matters (And How to Perfect It) Retrieved from https://www.hubspot.com/careers-blog/why-your-handshake-matters-and-how-to-perfect-it

26. Science of People (n.d) How to Read People Through Their Eye Movements and Uncover Hidden Emotions. Retrieved from https://www.scienceofpeople.com/read-people-eyes/

27. Vanessa (2017) 15 Signs You're Insecure AF. Retrieved from https://www.thetalko.com/15-signs-youre-insecure-af/

28. Vancruze R, (2018). 7 Best Ways To Influence Other People. Retrieved from https://vancruzer.com/influence-other-people/

29. Vital M, (n.d) The 16 Personality Types by Myers-Briggs and Keirsey. Retrieved from https://blog.adioma.com/16-personality-types/

30. Western Mastery. (n.d) 9 Powerful Tips on How to Read People. Retrieved from https://www.westernmastery.com/2018/03/11/tips-read-people/amp/

31. Wargo E. (n.d) How Many Seconds to a First Impression? Retrieved from https://www.psychologicalscience.org/observer/how-many-seconds-to-a-first-impression

32. Wikipedia (2019) Maslow's hierarchy of needs. Retrieved from https://en.wikipedia.org/wiki/Maslow%27s_hierarchy_of_needs

33. Wikipedia (2019). Face perception. Retrieved from https://en.wikipedia.org/wiki/Face_perception

ENNEAGRAM

Introduction

In this book you will find detailed descriptions about nine types of personalities. These personalities are what make up the Enneagram theory. Through these personalities, you will not only be able to understand yourself better, but your friends, partners, family, and co-workers.

This book can help start your journey to self-discovery. You will be able to learn your strengths, weaknesses, and how you can turn your weaknesses into strengths. You will learn about the highs of your personality and its lows. All this information will help to transform you into the best person you can become.

This book starts out by explaining what the Enneagram theory is. You will see a few of its diagrams, such as the Enneagram itself and its center points. You will get a brief introduction of the nine personality types and the 27 subtypes, as each personality type consists of three subtypes. You will also learn the benefits of the Enneagram theory.

Starting in chapter 2, you will begin to learn about the types of individual personalities. We will start with the first type of personality, which is the perfectionist. In chapter 3, you will learn about the helper. We will then look into the achiever in chapter 4. Chapter 5 will look at the individualist, which is the fourth personality type. The fifth personality type will be discussed in chapter 6, which is = the investigator. I will talk about the loyalist, in other words the sixth personality type, in chapter 7. The seventh personality type, which is the enthusiast, will be discussed in chapter 8. Chapter 9 will inform you about the protector. And finally, chapter 10 will focus on the ninth personality type, which is the mediator or peacemaker.

Chapter 11 is a special chapter as it focuses on the Enneagram test, which you can take for free online. However, you can always take the time to spend money taking the test elsewhere. This chapter will describe the test, give you a summary of the types, subtypes, and outline the difference between the Enneagram and the Myer-Briggs test.

By the end of this book, you should be able to understand the basics of the Enneagram theory. You should not only know which personality type you have but also be able to identify your strengths, weaknesses, and how you work with other personalities. From this book, you will also be able to identify if you sit at a healthy, average, or unhealthy level of integration. Once you identify your level, you will be able to find ways to help you reach the healthiest level so that you can become the best person you can be.

The Enneagram is more than a test that allows you to learn what numbered personally you have. It is a test that can give you the information you need in order to make sure you feel your life is being fulfilled to its fullest. At this point, I feel it is important to make sure you realize that everyone makes mistakes and no one is perfect. There are a couple of personalities in the Enneagram that struggle with imperfections. If you fall within one of these personalities, the first step you need to take is to realize that it is okay to be wrong, to struggle, and to not always be happy. However, it is also important to remember your mindset. No matter what personality you have, you will need to keep the right frame of mind if you want to remain at a healthy level with your personality.

Chapter 1
The Theory of Enneagram

No one is 100% certain where the Enneagram theory started. Some people believe it can be traced back mathematically, while others state it started through spirituality and Christianity. Plotinus, a Greek philosopher who lived in 200 A.D, spoke of nine principles of the human personality. Ramon Llull, a mathematician from the 13th century also spoke on nine personality types (Cloete, n.d.).

However, no matter how far back you trace the Enneagram theory, you will find an evolution devoted to it. Today, the Enneagram theory is a diagram which looks to identify a person's personality. However, many psychologists have also used this theory to identify people in large groups (Cloete, n.d.).

How it Works

One of the distinctive factors about the Enneagram theory is it doesn't put people into a box. Within the nine main types of personalities are 27 subtypes. On top of this, in each personality there are wings, lines, and other factors that help determine your unique personality (Cloete, n.d.). While the theory and diagram might seem complicated at first, as it is complex, it becomes easier to understand it the more you learn the details about the types, subtypes, and how the theory works in general.

Diagrams

The Enneagram Diagram

- 9 The Peacemaker
- 8 The Challenger
- 1 The Reformer
- 7 The Enthusiast
- 2 The Helper
- 6 The Loyalist
- 3 The Achiever
- 5 The Investigator
- 4 The Individualist

In order to help you understand the diagram of the Enneagram, you will want to look at it step by step. This will help you better understand and follow the basic structure of the Enneagram. For instance, you can start by looking at the diagram as a circle. Around this circle, you will see the numbers nine through one. While the numbers are numerical, if you go counter-clockwise, they are also placed in a systematic order, which is why nine is at the top. Each of these nine numbers represents a personality type, which you can identify in the diagram above.

People often get confused about the lines within the circle. As you can see, there are a variety of lines which go from one number to the next. These are the lines that guide you to your personality and your personality's wings. Again, if you take the lines one by one, you will gain a better understanding of the Enneagram.

First, take a look at numbers nine, six, and three. You will notice that when they are connected, they create an equilateral triangle. From there, you will want to look at the connections of numbers through six points which construct an irregular hexagram. You will want to make sure you follow the order below as the points have to be followed in this order.

1. number 1 connects to 4
2. number 4 connects to 2
3. number 2 connects to 8
4. number 8 connects to 5
5. number 5 connects to 7
6. number 7 connects to 1

When looking at the lines within the Enneagram, you will find that there are arrows which lead you to the following number.

9 Types + 27 Subtypes

You should never think that your personality will fall under just one type of personality. In fact, you will find pieces of your personality in all of the other personalities. However, you should also find the primary number associated with your personality. This number will represent the biggest part of your personality. Remember, the Enneagram is meant to take you out of a box, not put you into one. This is why your personality will be scattered throughout the diagram, but you will have one primary number.

In this section, I will run through the nine types and 27 subtypes that can form your personality. I will not go through these types and subtypes in detail within this section. Instead, the following chapters will be dedicated to each one of the nine types, where I will further discuss the types, subtypes, and other factors in detail.

The nine personality types of the Enneagram are as follows (Berkers, n.d.):

1. The Perfectionist
2. The Helper
3. The Achiever
4. The Individualist
5. The Investigator
6. The Loyalist
7. The Enthusiast
8. The Protector
9. The Mediator

There are a total of 27 subtypes within these nine personality types. There are three main categories that hold these subtypes. These categories are social, self-preservation, and one-on-one (Cloete, n.d.).

The social category focuses on how we get along with other people and our social instincts. It outlines how we maintain relationships and how we work with others. The social category also focuses on how we strive to do the best we can for other people (Cloete, n.d.).

The self-preservation category focuses on how well we preserve our body and mind. It relates to the ways we manage stress and other life events. It is the category that focuses on our emotions. This category looks at ways for us to do our best when it comes to preserving ourselves mentally, physically, and emotionally (Cloete, n.d.).

The one-on-one category focuses on the legacies we want to leave for future generations. Everyone, whether it is within your family or in the world, wants to be remembered when they leave this earth. This category focuses on how we take control of these types of situations. It further dives into our more personal one-on-one relationships with people and environmental factors. Through this category, we can determine what we want to leave behind and how we want to do our best while still on this earth (Cloete, n.d.).

Each personality type has one subtype within the social, self-preservation, and one-on-one category. To gain a better understanding of this, as it is complex, I will list each personality type with its category and subtype below. I will go into each subtype in detail later.

1. The Perfectionist

Social: Not adaptable

Self-preservation: Worry

One-on-one: Zeal

2. The Helper

Social: Ambition

Self-preservation: Privilege

One-on-one: Seduction

3. The Achiever

Social: Prestige

Self-preservation: Security

One-on-one: Charisma

4. The Individualist

Social: Shame

Self-preservation: Tenacity

One-on-one: Competition

5. The Investigator

Social: Totem

Self-preservation: Castle

One-on-one: Confident

6. The Loyalist

Social: Duty

Self-preservation: Warmth

One-on-one: Intimidation

7. The Enthusiast

Social: Sacrifice

Self-preservation: Network

One-on-one: Fascination

8. The Protector

Social: Solidarity

Self-preservation: Satisfaction

One-on-one: Possession

9. The Mediator

Social: Participation

Self-preservation: Appetite

One-on-one: Fusion

Center Points

Beyond the numbers and lines, the diagram is also divided into three triads or centers, which are heart, head, and body. These centers will further develop your personality by explaining your go-to emotions.

1. Heart Center

The Heart Center

The heart center focuses on numbers four, three, and two. Because the heart is often thought to be the leader of truth and emotions, these numbers represent someone who is usually more sensitive and strongly believes that we have to be honest about who we are. People who fall into the heart center feel a strong connection to the truth.

The go-to emotion for the heart center is shame. They are very concerned with their image and how other people view them. In fact, they are never truly happy with themselves unless they are able to see themselves through another person's eyes.

Like with the other two centers, the heart center has its strengths and weaknesses, however, these strengths and weaknesses will be determined based on which personality type you have. For example, type four's strengths will be different from type two's ("Heart Triad," n.d.).

Wing Points

The wing points are the parts of your personality which spread out to your two adjacent personality types (Cloete, n.d.). While these two types are not as big as your main personality type, they are important because they will balance out your personality. For instance, if you have a point four personality type, your adjacent type might be a point three. These other types are sometimes known to contradict a person's personality but are important, so we can completely understand the whole of someone's personality. In fact, this is why there are tests and theories like the Enneagram. Not only does it allow us to get to know ourselves better, but it can help people, such as psychologists, who are trying to get to know us so they can help us too.

The question that a lot of people ask is whether we all have one wing or two wings. While this has brought on some controversy, many people believe that we do have two wings. Each point adjacent to our main personality type is one of our wings. Therefore, if you have a type nine personality, your wings will be type one and type eight. But, other people state this is not true and everyone has only one wing. There are other people who state that your wings are not specific to a certain personality type. They believe that because our personality has pieces from every number, then we have our main type and every other type is a wing to our personality, meaning we would have eight wings.

One important note to make about having different wings is that some wings are more dominant than others. If you haven't taken the Enneagram test yet, you will notice that when you get your results, they are laid out in a graph. This graph starts with your main personality as the strongest and then lists the other types of personalities from strongest to weakest. Most results will list all nine personality types.

Lines

One of the hardest parts of the Enneagram theory for people to understand is the lines within the theory. While I discussed the lines before, such as how they connect to the point, I will take this time to give you a bit more information on what the lines mean.

These lines are called the lines of influence or lines of movement (Cloete, n.d.). They are the way you will trace your personality through the Enneagram. Even though we have a main personality type, we can move around between the lines. Our main type will remain the same, however, the situations we go through in life and other factors will influence our journey on the lines throughout the Enneagram.

There are two types of lines. There is the line of stress and the line of growth. When you look at your main personality type on the Enneagram, you will see two lines with arrows. One arrow will be pointing away from your number type, which is called the line of growth. The other arrow will be pointing towards your number type and this is referred to as the line of stress.

When you think of the line of growth, you can think of releasing yourself from your unhealthy personality types. This is the line which moves us towards healthier parts of a personality. While we move along this line, we will release our stresses in life and move towards self-actualization (Cloete, n.d.).

The line of stress is the opposite of the line of growth. This line focuses on how we feel when we are under pressure or stressed. Often, these instances will make us pick up unhealthy lifestyle habits. At the same time, we can work to change the negatives into positives, which will often help balance us out as individuals (Cloete, n.d.).

Levels of Integration

Levels of integration are also known as levels of integration. Within each personality type, there are other pieces which make up the personality. These are similar to your behaviors, motivations, and attitude. Basically, these are the pieces which help make up your whole personality, similar to how pieces of the puzzle come together to create the whole puzzle.

When you start to understand these levels, you will come to realize that when people are changing, such as feeling more relaxed one moment and then anxious the next, they are going through different levels within their personality.

There are three levels of integration, which are healthy, average, and unhealthy (Cloete, n.d.). When people exhibit an unhealthy level of integration, they let their fears or other emotions control them. When people are at an average level of integration, the core problem is still a driving force in their behavior, however, they are able to let go of some core issues. When people are at a healthy level of integration, they can let go of the core emotions as they understand why these are occurring. This helps them move on, so they can find a healthier way to manage life stresses and situations. In a sense, they move beyond the limitations they believed they had.

Within these levels of integration are other levels and numbers associated with each level. Each level has three numbers, which correlate to how well the personality performs within its level of integration. These smaller levels are as follows:

In the healthy level, you can be a level one, two or three. Level one is at the level of a libertarian. Level two is at the level of psychological capacity and level three is at the level of social value ("How The System Works," n.d.).

In the average level, you can be a level four, five, or six. Level four is the level representing social role or imbalance. Level five is at the level of interpersonal control. Level six is at the level of overcompensation ("How The System Works," n.d.).

In the unhealthy level, you can be a level seven, eight, or nine. Level seven is a level of violation. Level eight is at the level of compulsion and obsession. Level nine is at the level of pathological destructiveness ("How The System Works," n.d.).

Benefits of the Enneagram

People often turn to the Enneagram to learn more about their personality for many reasons. While some people are curious about their personality type, other people want to know so they can better understand themselves or another person. Psychologists and other professionals often use the Enneagram to help them better understand their patients.

There are several benefits which can come from the Enneagram. Not only can this theory and test benefit people on an individual level, but also as a group. Furthermore, the Enneagram can also benefit people on an organizational level.

Individual Level Benefits

- Help people understand why they are dealing with certain behavioral or emotional problems.
- Help people gain insight into their personality so they can understand themselves better.

- The Enneagram can help increase a person's confidence and motivation.
- The Enneagram can help increase a person's compassion for others.
- People can start to understand their previous behavioral patterns.
- The Enneagram can help people grow in general as they begin to understand their personality better.

Group Level Benefits

- The Enneagram can help decrease conflict within a group.
- It can also help each group member understand where another group member stands, why people act in certain ways, and where each member's strengths and weaknesses are.
- The Enneagram can help improve business processes.
- It can strengthen communication between team members, which will enhance other areas of the group.

Organizational Level Benefits

- The Enneagram can help limit the political atmosphere of an organization.
- It can improve the organization's leadership as a whole.
- The Enneagram can help the organization improve the emotions and fears associated with change.

The Enneagram is so much more than a diagram with lines, numbers, and arrows. It can also do more than to explain a person's personality. As you can see in the benefits above, the

Enneagram can help people advance in many areas of their personal and professional life. Furthermore, the Enneagram can continue to help you as you develop through life's different stages.

Chapter 2
The Perfectionist

The first type of personality is the perfectionist, also often called the reformer. Every personality type has a set of words which accurately describe the personality. While you will always want to read through your personality type description, you can also gain an idea of your personality through these few words. For the perfectionist, the descriptive words are perfectionistic, self-controlled, purposeful, and principled.

What is the Perfectionist

When people think of the word perfectionist, they automatically think of a person who is driven, controlling, and needs to make sure everything is always right. While all of this is true about this personality type, like with all other personalities, there are levels of integration. These levels give a range of how healthy or unhealthy a person's personality is. For example, someone with a perfectionist personality who is at an unhealthy level won't listen to someone who contradicts what he or she believes. However, if the type two personality is at a healthy level, then the perfectionist personality is tolerant, accepting, and understands that while he or she wants to be as perfect as possible, perfection is not possible to achieve ("Type One," n.d.).

The true meaning of someone with a type one personality is that they have a very clear concept of what is right and wrong. They understand rules and ethics and think they should be followed thoroughly. At the same time, they want to see positive change and will do what they feel they need to do in order to make this change happen ("Type One," n.d.).

People with a type one personality have a strong fear of making mistakes. This is why they often take more time in completing a task. They need to make sure they are doing everything as perfectly as they can so mistakes will be limited. They often feel like everything needs to be in a certain order and can maintain high standards. Some of their flaws include not having patience, becoming too controlling, and resentful ("Type One," n.d.).

The perfectionists' biggest fear is corruption. While there are many reasons for this, one of the biggest is that they see corruption as unorderly and lacking control. When there is corruption, ethical standards are not followed and the conditions are not improving ("Type One," n.d.).

The biggest desire for a perfectionist is to be the best person possible. The perfectionist wants to be a good person overall, even if he or she exhibits personality traits of impatience and withdraws from other people. These traits are often used as a defense mechanism to help the type one manage their perfectionist traits. Type one also wants to see a well-balanced world around them.

Some people who are known to have type one personalities are Katherine Hepburn, Maggie Smith, Tina Fey, Hilary Clinton, Michelle Obama, Joan of Arc, Nelson Mandela, Jerry Seinfeld, Prince Charles, Jimmy Carter, and Kate Middleton ("Type One," n.d.).

People who have type one personality feel the need to have a mission to accomplish. Not only do they have a mission to focus on, but they will also do whatever they can to fulfill this mission. At the same time, they feel the need to justify their actions to themselves. They will do this by asking themselves questions to why this mission is important and conducting research. If they decide their actions are justified, they become very passionate and work hard to make improvements.

The type one personality won't often let themselves stray from their mission or responsibilities ("Type One," n.d.). Because of this, they can become resentful towards others or the conditions. This can often make the perfectionist seem controlling and unable to adapt to his or her surroundings. However, this is generally not true. The problem is because the perfectionist is struggling to improve conditions, they become frustrated and act out aggressively or become resentful. This is the way many type one personalities manage their struggles, mistakes, and the realization that the situation is uncontrollable.

Level of Integration

As stated earlier, all personalities have a level of integration. These consist of three different levels, which are healthy, average, and unhealthy. Within these levels are smaller levels which range from one to nine. The healthy level consists of levels one through three. The moderate level consists of levels four through six, and the unhealthy level consists of levels seven through nine. Level one means a type one personality at its best. Of course, the level will either increase or decrease depending on how the type one personality deals with his or her environmental situations. This means that when a personality reaches an unhealthy level, such as nine, he or she is at their worst.

Healthy Level

When a type one personality is at level one, they are performing at their best. They have found ways to manage their stress during situations that keeps them from becoming too aggressive and controlling. While they don't always manage everything perfectly, they realize that this is fine because perfection doesn't truly exist. However, this won't keep them from continuing to try. They also realize that they cannot control various environmental factors or what other people do. Therefore, they feel calmer when things don't go as planned. They think that as long as they perform their best, they are successful. They know that as long as they are mindful of the moment, they will be able to see and give others the truth (Cloete, n.d.).

Perfectionists at level two healthy level continue to work to improve themselves as they know they can be better. At this level, the type one will know what is right from wrong. Furthermore, they will understand ethics in all environments, from a working standpoint to religious ethics. They remain strong when it comes to their own moral values and strive to become self-disciplined. They are also very responsible, mature, and rational about circumstances ("Type One," n.d.).

A level three type one is at a lower healthy level. They still maintain a healthy way of keeping their aggression controlled in most situations. They strive to continue to do their best. They are rational and very concerned about ethics and making sure they are followed. These levels tend to make great teachers because of the belief that they have a higher purpose to make sure others see the truth. They also believe in fairness, even within state and federal laws ("Type One," n.d.).

Average Level

The highest level for a type one under the average level is a level four. People who are at this level can't always control their behaviors over their emotions. They believe that it is up to them to improve society's conditions, which is a belief they are very passionate about. Unlike the perfectionists at a healthy level, they don't always think rationally about their actions and can sometimes find themselves resentful or aggressive. This usually is shown through telling people that what they are doing is wrong and explaining how things should be instead (Cloete, n.d.).

A perfectionist, who is at a level five, is often considered a "workaholic." They strive to make sure everything has an order, including their emotions. While they do tend to become overly emotional, especially when they make mistakes, they do their best to keep these emotions hidden from other people. Like most perfectionists, they are known to have a strong sense of what is right and wrong, however, they can also be impressionable. This can cause them to follow people who won't help them achieve their order and in turn they will make mistakes. When this happens, the type one can become resentful (Cloete, n.d.).

A level six perfectionist has strong opinions and is highly critical of other people and themselves. Type one personalities at the lowest average level don't watch their reactions as well as other perfectionists do. Therefore, they are often deemed to be angry and impatient. Furthermore, they are known to scold people who they believe are doing wrong. These perfectionists like to have things done their way and don't believe that any other way is correct (Cloete, n.d.).

Unhealthy Level

An unhealthy level for a type one personality is a level seven. People who are in this category are often referred to as bullies. They are people who believe that no one else is right, except for them. In fact, some people refer to perfectionists at this level as narcissists. They can become very angry and lack patience when things aren't as they should be ("Type One," n.d.).

A level eight perfectionist often becomes so focused on what wrong things other people are doing that they lose track of what wrong things they are doing themselves. When this happens, they can find themselves doing the opposite of what they think is right. They tend to be very illogical thinkers and can have trouble problem-solving as they tend to do what they feel is right instead of what is actually right. They don't have a clear sense of morals and values as much as other type one personalities above them do ("Type One," n.d.).

A level nine represents a type one being at their lowest level of integration. They struggle in several areas for various reasons. Some perfectionists at this level are diagnosed with various mental illnesses, such as severe depression and obsessive-compulsive disorder. Unfortunately, suicidal thoughts and suicide are also high at this level (Cloete, n.d.).

Subtypes of the Perfectionist

Social Category is Non-Adaptable

Perfectionists are non-adaptable because they follow the rules and morals of what is right. They also believe that it is their job to make things right, if they see them as wrong, and are not typically flexible in this area. One of their biggest motivations to make things right is to make sure there is fairness (Cloete, n.d.).

Self-Preservation Category is Worry

Perfectionists spend a lot of time worrying because they want to make sure everything they do and everything that is around them is right. Therefore, they not only worry about their actions but the actions of others. This can cause them to feel anxious, especially when they believe that things aren't going as planned. Part of this is because they need to make sure they are well-prepared for their current situations. This not only includes making sure everything is in an orderly fashion, but also noticing every single detail which other people may miss (Cloete, n.d.).

One-on-One Category is Zeal

Zeal is known as a countertype. Depending on the healthy, average, and unhealthy level of a type one personality, it will determine how well they manage their personal relationships. Because many believe they are right, they feel authorized to tell others they are wrong. This can often cause all sorts of conflict when it comes to close relationships (Cloete, n.d.).

Relationships with Other Types

Type one is compatible with every other personality type. No matter what type they come in contact with, they can work with the individual. Of course, each personality will bring its own positivity and challenges to the relationship. For example, when it comes to a type one working with another type one, they will often run into conflict because they both strongly believe that they know only one of them is right. Therefore, if they don't agree on something, they will struggle to find any type of happy-medium. Perfectionists are very compatible with types nine, two, five, seven, and eight. They will struggle more with types one, three, four, and six. However, all this will also depend on the level of integration a type one associates with, along with the level of integration the other personality type associates with ("Relationships (Type Combinations)," n.d.).

Wing Types

The two wing personalities for the perfectionist are type nine and type two. Both of these wings will give the perfectionist positives and challenges. The positives for type nine are their drive, helping perfectionists become more relaxed, becoming more considerate of other people, and understanding that other people can also be right. One of the challenges that type nine brings to type one is that they might neglect situations which are difficult and in turn self-neglect.

The positives which type two brings to the perfectionist are taking care of themselves, helping others, and having compassion for other people. The challenges type two can bring to type one are the feeling of being taken advantage of and becoming overly sensitive to what other people think about them (Cloete, n.d.).

Center Point

A type one personality falls under the body center (Cloete, n.d.). If you have a type one personality, you will internalize your anger. People who have type one personality are very self-critical and often hard on themselves to a fault. They don't criticize themselves harshly because they lack criticism, they do this because they don't want to show their anger externally. In fact, they often try their hardest to make sure they don't show anger towards other people.

Type one's strengths:

- Hard-working
- Honest
- Independent
- Reliable
- Accountable

Type one's weaknesses:

- Rigidness
- Overly-critical
- Judgmental
- Resentful

How to Grow Personally

Whether you believe you are at the healthiest level of integration or close to the highest, there is always room for personal growth in your professional and personal life. Below are several pieces of advice which can help you grow as someone with a type one personality.

Keep the Right Mindset

While this will take time and how much time depends on what level you are currently at. Of course, the higher the level, the more time it will take. When I talk about the right mindset, I am talking about several characteristics, such as patience for others, remaining calm, and keeping your emotions in check. Furthermore, most type one personalities think they are always right, which can cause them to become emotional if people don't follow their ways or prove that they are wrong.

Perfectionists are known to be great teachers. However, they often struggle with teaching because they lack patience and consideration for people who do something wrong. But, if you have the right mindset, you will find that you can be an exceptional teacher; you will just have to make sure you have the patience, are able to deal with people who make mistakes, realize that you are not always right, and also realize that perfectionism is not completely possible. While reaching all these factors might seem impossible to you, especially if you have a lower level of integration, you do possess the motivation and drive to make sure you succeed if you become passionate about acquiring the right mindset.

You will want to remain calm. Perfectionists often struggle with keeping their emotions in check. Many perfectionists struggle with keeping their emotions in check because they are highly rigid about how things need to be done. Their primary emotion is anger, which means that they will show more anger than any other emotion. This can cause more problems within the issues already established. Therefore, the calmer you are able to remain, the more you will succeed in keeping your emotions, especially anger, in check. Once you are able to control your anger, you will find it is easier to control other emotions (Cloete, n.d.).

Chapter 3
The Helper

Type two personality is known as the helper and the giver. This personality type is one which focuses on helping others. Some of the primary words used to describe the helper are people-pleaser, demonstrative, possessive, and generous. The stress line for the helper shifts from a type two to a type eight, while the growth line shifts from a type two to a type four.

What is the Helper?

Stevie Wonder, Danny Glover, Martin Sheen, Elizabeth Taylor, and Richard Thomas (John boy Walton) are all considered to have a type two personality. People who have this personality type are typically warm and caring individuals. Not only are they generous but they are highly compassionate and don't tend to pass judgment. They are driven by their need to help others and can often be found in professions such as non-profits and volunteering at soup kitchens ("Type Two," n.d).

A type two's biggest desire is to be loved while their biggest fear is the feeling of being unwanted or unloved. In fact, one of the biggest reasons they focus on helping people is to fulfill this desire. They believe that the more they help people, the more people will enjoy their company and care about them. It is this feeling that makes helpers take so much time out of their day to make sure they are fulfilling their mission of helping other people.

People quickly see that type two personalities have big hearts. Therefore, they are drawn to helpers. Unfortunately, this can also cause problems because there are many people who are more interested in taking advantage of helpers. For many type two personalities, this becomes a problem because they don't often have the courage to defend themselves against people who take advantage of them. While some are able to defend themselves, many others continue to help people because they fear that people will not like them if they don't help..

Individuals with a type two personality are similar to a sponge. They tend to soak up emotions from other people, which can cause them to feel overwhelmed by all the different emotions. If they don't know how to release these emotions, they can be prone to emotional outbursts as this allows them to relieve the pressure. Because of this, it is important for them to find a balance between feeling loved by other people and loving themselves. No matter how much love you feel from someone else, it will never substitute self-love.

Levels of Integration

Healthy Level

A level one type two is the best level that you can reach. These types of people don't ever think that they should be rewarded for helping. People who reach this level are known to be selfless and help people because they feel true unconditional love for others, even those who have wronged them or others in the past. They believe that it is a privilege to be accepted by other people and be a part of their lives (Cloete, n.d.).

A level two type two is similar to a level one, however, these types sometimes believe that they should receive some help back. While they are extremely warm, compassionate, and caring individuals, they also hold more realistic expectations of how people can take advantage of them. However, they don't always act when they think they are being taken advantage of ("Type Two," n.d.).

A level three type two tends to take care of themselves as much as they take care of other people. They like to maintain a good balance, however, if it comes down to either help themselves or another person, they will help the other person first. Like the higher type two personalities, they are very nurturing, warm, caring, and generous. They believe that everyone has an ultimate good about them (Cloete, n.d.).

Average Level

A level four type two will have a lot of helpful qualities and good intentions. They don't often feel that they are entitled to help from other people. However, they also brag about how helpful they are. They believe that people should acknowledge their behavior and reward them. However, they don't often look for materialistic rewards, they would rather receive a reward through praise (Cloete, n.d.).

A level five type two personalities expect a return from the people they help. Those at a level five also tend to feel so strongly towards helping people that they can come off as more pushy than helpful (Cloete, n.d.). They don't fully understand the line between being helpful and becoming overly helpful.

A level six type two personality can also become overbearing when they are helping others (Cloete, n.d.). They believe that they do deserve rewards, however, they are not always open about this belief. They feel that they are irreplaceable and have a strong sense of self-importance.

Unhealthy Level

When a helper is at a level seven, they can often be manipulative. While they still like to help other people, they also feel more entitled to help (Cloete, n.d.). For example, if a type two personality helps you with raking your lawn, he or she will tell you how much you owe him or her the next time they need or want something. Unlike healthy level type two's, this unhealthy level will often think that he or she shouldn't complete any actions for free. In a sense, level seven type two's always want something back, a reward of sorts, for their helpful behavior.

A level eight type two is similar to a level seven but often feels entitled to any type of favor they want from someone else (Cloete, n.d.). These favors can come in the form of money, house work, or sexual activities. Someone who ranks at level eight for a type two personality is generally not shy about asking what they want. Furthermore, they don't possess the warm and caring personality that the majority of type two personalities do when they are asking for help.

A level nine type two is the lowest level that a type two personality can have. Similar to the other unhealthy levels, they feel highly entitled to favors and jobs performed by other people (Cloete, n.d.). However, they will also justify their behavior and the way they treat people because of the helpful nature of their personality. They believe that because they treat people with kindness, they are able to act towards a person how they wish.

Subtypes of the Helper

Social Category is Ambition

Type two personalities have a lot of ambition and can often be seen taking on leadership roles. They like to feel like they are important and needed, therefore, they will find people and organizations who need them. Because of their caring and helpful personality, people are quickly attracted to them, which easily helps them engage groups of people. This can also allow the helper to get what they want out of the groups, such as completing tasks or getting more help from others (Cloete, n.d.).

However, type two personalities often feel uncomfortable when they are alone. This happens for several reasons, one being that they feel they are not doing whatever they can to help someone. Therefore, many professionals agree that helpers will use their personality in order to block out their uncomfortable feelings. The busier they are, the less likely they will be able to feel what they don't want to feel (Cloete, n.d.).

Self-Preservation Category is Privilege

This is the countertype of type two. In fact, they are often mistaken to be a type seven personality. A type two can often cause other personalities to feel like they need to be protected because of their helpful nature. Because of this, type two is often considered to be a little child-like and shy. They don't mind feeling like they are being protected, however, they also don't want to become too dependent on someone else. They feel that their sense of self-protection is a privilege, so they treat it with care. Furthermore, they have a big fear of rejection, which makes them feel like they have to protect themselves more than someone else would (Cloete, n.d.).

One-on-One Category is Seduction

Type two personalities are very giving, compassionate, and thought to be extremely selfless, however, this doesn't mean that they don't want to feel important to someone. No matter what level a type two personality is, whether healthy, average, or unhealthy, they still feel a need to receive compassion and love from someone. Therefore, when type two personalities get into an intimate relationship, they start to feel this connection very strongly. They will often use the caring and loving parts of their personality towards their partner so they can feel these emotions back.

Once the type two personality gets into a very close relationship, they can start to feel very passionate. Of course, this passion comes with positives and negatives. For example, one positive is they will begin to feel more comfortable and trust their partner. However, one negative is they will start to have trouble taking no for an answer. In fact, they might find it hard to set and follow limits (Cloete, n.d.).

Relationships with Other Types

Type two personalities tend to get along with type one and type three the best because these personalities are type two's wings. However, they also get along with generally any type of personality. But, of course, they will struggle with some personalities more than others. For example, type two and type five struggle with getting along. While they will eventually get along, type two views type five as a challenging personality that is often difficult to form a relationship with ("Relationships (Type Combinations)," n.d.).

Some of these types are better off as friends and co-workers rather than to be in a romantic relationship. For example, type four and type two get along exceptionally well and often create a very warm and compassionate relationship. However, they make better friends than romantic partners.

Wing Types

The two wings for type two personality are type one and type three. Both of these wings not only help type two to manage their personality better, but also involves challenges. When it comes to positives, the type one will bring more balance to the type two by having them help everyone and not their favorite people. Furthermore, type one helps them establish boundaries so people don't consistently take the type two for granted. Type one can also help type two improve their environment. When it comes to challenges, type one can make type two have unrealistic expectations, become too hard on themselves for mistakes, become sensitive to criticism, and cause them to neglect themselves (Cloete, n.d.).

The type three personality can provide type two advantages by helping them with their focus, self-esteem, and the ability to adapt to other people and their surroundings. The challenges that type two faces with a type three wing is the act of neglecting themselves because they become too focused on their work and become selective when it comes to helping people (Cloete, n.d.).

Center Point

If you have a type two personality, you will sit under the heart center point and externalize your feelings of shame (Cloete, n.d.). This is often what makes you become the best person you can be, which is why you are often seen as helpful and supportive. In a sense, you use your shame in order to create a better person and help others. This provides you with an image of yourself as being needed and well-liked, which makes you feel better about your shame.

Type two's strengths:

- Helpful
- Generous
- Supportive
- Caring
- Relationships
- Sensitive

Type two's weaknesses:

- Dependent
- Demanding
- Prideful
- Privileged
- Intrusive

How to Grow Personally

Remember to Ask People What They Need

A type two personality wants to help people in any way possible. Because of this, they often forget to ask the person what type of help they really need or want. Sometimes people don't want to receive the help you are giving them, which means you aren't really helping them at all. It is important for other people, and yourself, to make sure that you are using your energy on the people who really want the help. Don't be afraid to ask them if you can help them in any way. If people really need the help, they will let you know. If they tell you that they don't need your help, just let them know that you are available if they ever do. Often, when people know that you are available to help them is all they need to hear to feel loved and cared about (Cloete, n.d.).

Be Conscious of Your Motives

As stated above, there are a few levels of type two personalities that expect certain things in return and start to feel entitled to being treated well because of the way they treat others. This is an example of poor interior motives, which is something that you should improve on if you begin to feel this way. While everyone has the internal feeling of wanting to receive some of the help and compassion they give to others, when you start to feel like you deserve this compassion and love because of your actions, you should take a step back and rethink your motives. You want to help other people because it's a part of your personality. You want to be compassionate to others because you hold a special personality that strongly advocates compassion. You want to use these important pieces of your personality to strengthen the lives of others and not cause harm (Cloete, n.d.).

Don't Forget About Yourself

You might think that you deserve rewards because you are forgetting to take care of yourself. This is often a weakness for someone with a type two personality. No matter what personality you have, it is important to make sure that you take time for yourself and give yourself the care you need, so you can live a happy and healthy life. Type two personalities often forget to take care of themselves because they are so fixated on taking care of other people. However, this can harm you in the end. Therefore, it is important to make sure to give yourself some care and pampering time just as you would for anyone else. Doing so will allow you to spread your unconditional love to others easier (Cloete, n.d.).

Chapter 4
The Achiever

The stress line for type three personality runs from point three to point nine and its growth line runs from three to point six. The primary words used to describe an achiever are driven, adaptable, image-conscious, and excelling. Some famous achievers are O.J. Simpson, Paul McCartney, Madonna, Muhammad Ali, Will Smith, Bill Clinton, and Michael Jordan ("Type Three," n.d).

What is the Achiever?

Type three personalities are known to be very driven. They are considered workaholics and tend to be concerned about what other people think of them. They are known to be ambitious, energetic, diplomatic, and always looking at ways they can advance in their careers in life ("Type Three," n.d.).

An achiever's biggest fear is the feeling of being worthless internally and externally. Therefore, they will strive to become the best person possible. They want to do their best in their career field. Achievers also want other people to see how well they do in their career and other aspects of their life.

An achiever's desire is to feel worthwhile and valued. They often feel this way when they continue to reach their goals and remain ambitious to do their best. In fact, because they are so ambitious, people often look up to them. Many people believe that achievers are some of the most inspirational people because of everything they accomplish.

For achievers, there are many things that help them define their success. They use their status in their careers and their personal lives. They use their popularity as a way to measure success. At the same time, they also use their relationships with their friends, family, and co-workers to define their success ("Type Three," n.d.).

Most achievers tend to be considered popular because people want to be associated with them. Not only do they look up to them, but many other personalities believe that achievers can also help them accomplish their goals in life. In fact, out of all the personality types, the achiever is known to be the most well-liked.

However, the need to be successful is not just to fulfill their needs in life. In fact, most think that they won't get attention from other people unless they are successful. Like any other personality, type three wants to feel like they are needed and accepted by others. Therefore, they use their drive to become successful, believing this is how they will acquire this feeling from others.

Because of this, people with this type of personality can often forget about what they want in life. In fact, when they do is take a step back and realize they are neglecting themselves, because they have no idea what they truly want to get out of their life. This can lead type three personalities to a crossroad. While they want to continue to be successful, so other people give them what they desire most, they also realize they can't continue to neglect themselves. This is when a lot of issues arise for the achiever as they begin to strive to find a balance.

Levels of Integration

Healthy Level

The best level an achiever can reach is the first level. Achievers who are at a level one are completely honest with their accomplishments, which are often astounding to many people. They work hard and always put in as much effort as they can in everything they do. They are also known to be very charitable, gentle, and self-accepting. They have found a balance between showing people their success and taking care of themselves. Furthermore, they are known to be non-judgmental and want to help others achieve success as well (Cloete, n.d.).

An achiever at level two has high self-esteem and knows their value. However, they often don't admit their value to other people because this might make them seem arrogant. It's at the level two when achievers start paying attention to other people's opinions of them. So they can continue their success and become the best person they can be. They believe that people have to see them this way. Therefore, they don't believe in bragging about their accomplishments. In fact, they are known to be shy about what they accomplish in their lives. People see achievers at level two as very adaptable, charming, and generous (Cloete, n.d.).

A level three achiever is constantly focusing on doing the best they can for themselves and other people. They are often seen as a role model because of their drive and ability to succeed. However, most level three achievers do not know their true worth when it comes to their career and personal life. One reason for this is because they are always trying to better themselves. Therefore, no matter what they do, they think that they can do it even better. However, they do realize they are successful people as they are proud of the achievements they accomplish (Cloete, n.d.).

Average Level

At level four, achievers believe that their self-worth depends on the achievements they have made in life. They will continue to push themselves to do the best they can. At this point, achievers tend to forget about their own emotions and mentality when it comes to accomplishing their goals. While they are seen by others as being incredibly successful, they never believe they are truly that successful and continue to work harder. One reason for this is because the fear of failure is intense for a level four. They are constantly worried about how they failed or how they could fail, which gives them more energy to succeed (Cloete, n.d.).

An achiever at level five starts to become more worried about how they appear to other people. They will often ask people what they think or how they feel about them. When they are told, they take the person's answer to heart and do what they can to continue to improve themselves. At this level, achievers start to forget about what they want to completely focusing on what other people think they should do or what other people want to see them accomplish. Level five achievers begin to lose touch with their reality and forget about how they need to care for themselves first (Cloete, n.d.).

At level six, an achiever starts to promote themselves as much as possible. They spend a lot of their time bragging about their accomplishments and observing what other people think about what they accomplished. People at a level six also tend to lie about what they have accomplished because they need to make sure that they sound better than they really are. It is at this level they start to exhibit signs of narcissism and are believed to be very arrogant (Cloete, n.d.).

Unhealthy Level

At a level seven, an achiever's fear of being forgotten becomes so strong that they will do whatever they can to make sure people don't forget about them or their achievements. At this stage, they have to make sure that people continue to believe they are superior. In fact, at this level, they want people to think that they could never be as good as the achiever (Cloete, n.d.).

When an achiever is at level eight, they can become dishonest and manipulative. This is because they will start to believe they need to cover up their mistakes at all costs. This is also when they start to become jealous of other people who they believe are doing better then they are. In order to remain on top, they will start to deceive people into thinking that they are better than anyone else (Cloete, n.d.).

The lowest level for an achiever is level nine. At this level, achievers exhibit signs of psychopathic behavior or are considered to be narcissistic. Achievers who are a level nine will do whatever it takes to make sure they are the best and people believe they are the best, even if it means hurting someone in order to remain on top. Achievers who are a level nine will ruin someone else's happiness in order to gain what they want and accomplish their goals, or at least give people the illusion that they accomplished their goals (Cloete, n.d.).

Subtypes of the Achiever

Social Category is Prestige

Type three personalities are very concerned about their outward appearance. In fact, they sometimes become so concerned that they will cheat and lie in order to make themselves look more successful than they are. They are competitive by nature and will do what they can in order to gain the spotlight. At the same time, they are very talented and while they can be competitive, they also work well in groups. In fact, they are known to adjust to their social settings, which is one reason they are successful (Cloete, n.d.).

Self-Preservation Category is Security

Security is the countertype to the achiever. While they like to know what other people think of them and often base their success on their outward appearance, they don't want people to believe they care about what other people think. In a sense, achievers like to keep this a secret (Cloete, n.d.).

One-on-One Category is Charisma

Achievers compete for the spotlight, but at the same time, they can be very rational about the spotlight they get. Part of this is because of their security and not wanting to show that they want to be in the spotlight. Another part of this is because when achievers are at a healthy level of integration, they realize that it's not necessary that people know about all their achievements.

Furthermore, achievers are known to maintain good relationships. In fact, many people think that type three personalities are very supportive because they want to see other people succeed as well. This is especially true when achievers work in groups. Achievers often follow the belief that if the people they hang out with are successful, they too will become successful (Cloete, n.d.).

Relationships with Other Types

How well a type three gets along with other personalities will depend on the developmental level of the achiever. A type three who is around a level seven to nine will struggle to get along with a lot of other personalities because they tend to have high narcissistic tendencies and believe they are better than everyone else. However, for achievers who are in a more healthy or average level will be able to get along with almost any other personality type. However, the personality type that most achievers will deem a challenge is type six. However, they are able to work well together ("Relationships (Type Combinations)," n.d.).

Wing Types

The achiever's wings are personality types two and four. In regard to type two, the achiever receives several strengths, such as learning how to balance their work and personal life. Furthermore, type two personality helps type three realize that they can't use people, they have to value their thoughts and beliefs. Because of type two, achievers are able to strengthen their personal relationships, whether they are intimate or not. However, there are also challenges for type three. One of these challenges is that type two can make achievers strive for the approval of others. This can also cause the achievers to feel burnt-out because they work too hard to impress other people and become very critical of themselves when they think people don't value their achievements (Cloete, n.d.).

Type four teaches the achievers to value friendships with others. They help type three realize they have to be true to themselves in order to really achieve the success they want to achieve. At the same time, they help type three reach a sensitivity when it comes to the way other people are feeling. However, this can also become a challenge for achievers. A type four personality can also lead achievers to withdraw from people, which can cause them to become moody or irritated. Furthermore, this can lead them to think that people don't appreciate them and what they have accomplished. When achievers begin to think this way, they start to brag about their achievements and believe that people should be more appreciative and pay more attention to everything they have accomplished. Another negative that the type four wing can bring to a type three is force them to jump into relationships just because they are looking for something that's missing. For example, if a type three doesn't feel appreciated, they will strive to feel appreciation in their intimate relationship (Cloete, n.d.).

Center Point

A type three personality is part of the heart center (Cloete, n.d.). If you have a type three personality, you will understand who you are through the feedback of other people. This is because you are often out of touch with your own feelings, which makes getting a clear sense of who you are, or how well you do on something, difficult. As a type three, you find yourself resenting your feeling of shame, which can lead you to your strengths and weaknesses. For example, you change the shame you feel into success.

Type three's strengths:

- Strive for success
- Enthusiastic
- Practical
- Problem-solving
- Efficient
- Determined
- Competent

Type three's weaknesses:

- Overworked
- Competitive
- Image-driven
- Impatient
- Out of touch with your feelings

How to Grow Personally

Remember to Take Breaks

Because type three personalities are such high achievers and always looking at what they can accomplish next, they often forget to take care of themselves. This can easily wear a person out and cause them to feel emotionally, mentally, and physically exhausted. When this happens, they can easily fall from a level two or three to a level five or six. Therefore, it is essential that achievers remember to take breaks and to make sure they take time to care for their mental and emotional health.

While ambition and dedication to achieve your goals and become successful are great qualities, like any characteristics they can have negative effects. Some of these effects can harm you mentally, emotionally, and physically ("Type Three," n.d.). For example, you can drive yourself into exhaustion or you can start to feel majorly depressed because you do not take care of yourself. Whether it is working too hard or not taking time for yourself, you have to remember that you can only truly succeed if you are fully charged and ready. You don't have to take a lot of time to charge, in fact, just taking a quick break can help you feel recharged.

Remember Your Interests

Because achievers tend to focus so much on what other people think about them, they often forget about their own interests. Instead, they try to show interest in factors that other people find interesting and want them to achieve, even if the type three is not interested. While many achievers will continue to work towards this goal, because they want to show others they can achieve it, they can quickly start to feel a sense of worthlessness or depression because they are not working towards what they want to do ("Type Three," n.d.).

Because of this, it is important to make sure that what you are working towards is what you want to do, and not what someone else wants you to do. You have to have some type of interest in your work or else you will harm yourself mentally and emotionally. Instead of doing what you can to prove your accomplishments to others, you can start working with them.

This way, even if you are not fully interested in the task, you are with people who are and by working as a team, you will be able to remain successful.

Be Honest with Yourself

In order to truly be successful, you have to be honest with yourself and everyone else. Don't spend time to inflate your accomplishments. Instead, be honest with them. Let them know what you have really accomplished and what you didn't accomplish. The more realistic you are about your achievements, the more people are going to see you as a role model. People look up to others who are honest. If they find that you are constantly bragging about your accomplishments or lying about what you have completed, they are less likely to see you as successful and someone worth trusting ("Type Three," n.d.).

Chapter 5
The Individualist

The primary words used to describe an individualist are dramatic, expressive, temperamental, and self-absorbed. The growth line for a type four personality moves to a type one personality. The stress line moves from a type four to a type two personality. Some famous people with type four personalities include Johnny Depp, Kate Winslet, Amy Winehouse, Billie Holiday, Judy Garland, Anne Frank, and Hank Williams ("Type Four," n.d.).

What is the Individualist?

Type four personalities are known to be extremely sensitive to what is going on around them. They tend to feel emotions deeply. In fact, most feel emotions on a deeper level than other personalities. Of course, this can cause problems when it comes to a type four because they can have trouble controlling their feelings, which can become overwhelming. Because of this, the individualist will need to use certain techniques, so they can manage the stress of their emotions.

Because of how overwhelming emotions can be, the individualist will withdraw from society. They will usually have a select group of friends they regularly see and talk to, and they tend to withdraw from others. Their overwhelming emotions can also cause them to feel self—pity, melancholy, or become severely depressed. Just because type four personalities tend to withdraw from society, doesn't mean they want to be alone in their life. Unfortunately, because of their lack of social life, they often begin to feel this way which can increase their depression or internal sadness. At the same time, because individualists are concerned about their self-image, they will often become anxious when in a social setting. They are afraid of making a mistake that will cause people to judge them or think that they are socially awkward, which will deter them from social settings ("Type Four," n.d.).

The biggest struggle a type four has in regard to their emotions is letting go of the past. They often feel guilty over mistakes they have made, especially if it negatively affected their self-image. On top of this, they genuinely struggle with letting go of emotions. Therefore, type four personalities can hold on to emotions for years, if not longer.

Their main desire is to feel that they have significance ("Type Four," n.d.). They want to be sure they have an identity in the world and be able to understand themselves. When it comes to their biggest fear, which is also their strongest emotion, they worry about their identity and what special features they have. They want to do something special and become noticed. Therefore, they are often worried about their personal significance and fear that they have none.

The reason why this fear is so extreme for the individualist is because they know they aren't like other people. They believe they are different, which makes them believe that others cannot understand them. While they know they possess unique and one-of-a-kind talents, they also believe that they are uniquely flawed. Because of this, they tend to become more aware of their unique characteristics more than other people. They also make sure to take care of these characteristics more than most people.

Individualists believe that their unique characteristics are some of the most important features of their personality ("Type Four," n.d.).

Type four personalities are often motivated when they are able to express their individuality. They also like to see the beauty in the world and will often surround themselves with what they find beautiful. They also receive motivation when they are allowed to take care of themselves before they need to take care of someone else. However, they enjoy knowing that they are about to help other people ("Type Four," n.d.).

Other than becoming overwhelmed with emotions, individualists often think that they are missing something in their life. Unfortunately, they never fully grasp an idea of what they are missing. Therefore, they think it can be a variety of factors and will often try different careers or change aspects of their personality to figure out what is missing ("Type Four," n.d.). For example, some might think they don't have enough friends, so they will start to become more social. Other individualists might think that they are missing a piece of themselves, such as self-confidence, so they will start to increase their confidence.

A couple of the biggest problems individualists face with themselves is their lack of self-esteem and poor self-image. Both of these factors tend to negatively affect individualists in several ways throughout their life. For example, it can be what causes them to become socially withdrawn, not use their talent to its fullest potential, or become afraid to try something new out of fear of what it will do to their self-image. Because of this, they will often compensate by creating an idealized image of themselves. They use this image as someone they want others to see them as. They will also use this imaginary version of themselves to become the best person they can be.

Levels of Integration

Healthy Level

The highest level for an individualist is level one, which means that they are able to let go of their past emotions, realize they have a positive self-image, and are able to take all their life experiences and transform them into something special and valuable. These experiences are able to help them learn and grow, which is what they focus on when they are transforming. They also realize they are very unique and creative people, and are not shy about expressing themselves, whether it is through art, music, or writing (Cloete, n.d.).

At a level two, individualists are known to be extremely gentle, sensitive, and compassionate. They are aware that they internalize feelings deeply and use techniques in order to help themselves manage the feeling of becoming overwhelmed with emotion. They are comfortable with their self-image, but also believe that they still need to improve themselves. Furthermore, they still continue to search for who they really are (Cloete, n.d.).

An individualist who is at a level three, is honest with themselves and others. They are self-aware of their emotions but often overcome their overwhelming feeling with humor. In fact, they are known to not be very serious people because they tend to find humor in almost anything. Even if they think their self-image has drawn on some negativity, they realize that this happens because no one is perfect and people make mistakes.

Therefore, they are known to remain true to themselves (Cloete, n.d.).

Average Level

A type four who is at a level four tends to use their creative abilities to overcome their strong feelings. They are also known to be the most romantic individualists. Like others, they focus on creating a beautiful environment around them, even if they have to create a fantasy to do this. They are known to have an active imagination but do their best to remain true to their passionate emotions (Cloete, n.d.).

Individualists who are at a level five tend to take everything personally and have trouble separating what isn't aimed at them and what is. Because of this, they are perceived to be very self-absorbed people but, in reality, they are hypersensitive. They are also very self-conscious and shy, which makes it hard for them to become spontaneous. They are considered to be introverted. They often don't spend a lot of time in social settings because it helps them protect their self-image. Another reason they are introverted is because it allows them to control their emotions better because they are able to out their emotions (Cloete, n.d.).

A type four who is at a level six tends to focus more on self-pity because they realize they are different, which means they cannot live the same way as other people do. Because of this, they will often create a happier and healthier fantasy world. Other people tend to view a level six as self-indulgent and unproductive. At the same time, they are also viewed as dreamers and unique individuals (Cloete, n.d.).

Unhealthy Level

One of the unhealthy levels for a type four is a level seven. At this level, individualists tend to get very angry with themselves, which makes them become socially withdrawn. Because of this, they often struggle with depression. Furthermore, they start to feel ashamed by their overwhelming emotions, which makes them block out their emotions. A level seven will often struggle with daily functioning because they often feel exhausted. Individualists will start to reach this level when their fantasy world fails and they can no longer imagine a happier world for themselves (Cloete, n.d.).

A level eight often starts to feel tormented by their self-image. These individualists usually have very low self-esteem and often blame others for their problems. At this level, individualists tend to hate themselves and think melancholy. They will often push away anyone who tries to help them for several reasons, such as wanting to be alone or feeling like they don't deserve the help (Cloete, n.d.).

The highest level that individualists can reach is a level nine. Type four personalities who reach this level typically have problems with drugs and alcohol as this helps them cope with their morbid thoughts and low self-esteem. They often find themselves contemplating suicide and suffer from various mental diseases such as narcissistic and avoidant personality disorders (Cloete, n.d.).

Subtypes of the Individualist

Social Category is Shame

Shame is the basic emotion for a type four personality.

Therefore, this emotion shows up in their daily lives constantly. In fact, they can quickly make themselves feel guilty, which will cause them to also feel ashamed. While they are not competitive, they do like people telling them they are positively influencing other people in society. They like to know their self-worth as this helps them understand who they are. Socially, they are open to people when it comes to the shame they feel, which makes people admire and support individualists. This will often boost the confidence of a type four because they are quick to doubt themselves and their abilities (Cloete, n.d.).

Self-Preservation Category is Tenacity

Tenacity is the countertype for individualists and often makes people mistake them for a type one or type seven personality. Through self-preservation, type four personalities learn to live with their suffering, with some finding ways to overcome it. In fact, they often believe that it is their suffering which has made them stronger and able to manage various life circumstances. Because of this, they will often look for other people who they believe suffer in the same way they have so they can become a support system for them (Cloete, n.d.).

One-on-One Category is Competition

Type four personalities are not competitive when it comes to sports. Their competitive nature comes out when they have demands and want attention from other people in order to prove their self-worth. They become competitive when it comes to other people believing they are helpful, sensitive, compassionate, and generous individuals. Furthermore, individualists can become demanding when it comes to wanting people to listen to their emotions. In a sense, individualists want people to understand what they need and appreciate the struggles they face as sensitive people (Cloete, n.d.).

Relationships with Other Types

Depending on what level of integration individualists are in will influence how well they get along with other types. If they are at the healthiest level of integration, they can get along with nearly all the other personalities. However, when they are at a lower average and unhealthy level they will be less likely to have a healthy relationship with other personalities ("Relationships (Type Combinations)," n.d.).

Wing Types

One of the wings for type four personalities is type three. The advantages that the achievers bring to the individualists are helping them express their creative fantasies. Because of the type three personality, type four is able to balance their internal drama so that they can become more social. When they do reach their social setting, achievers will help them express their unique selves in a way that can engage other people. On top of this, type three will help the type four transform their life experiences in a positive way. The challenges that achievements bring to individualists are the feelings of having to hide their emotions and internalizing them as a way to control them. Achievers can also increase the feeling of sadness that type four personalities have because of the pressure individualists will feel towards achieving a certain level of success (Cloete, n.d.).

The second wing for individualists is type five. When it comes to the advantages that type five brings, it is teaching individualists to take things less personally. They also help them control their emotions and help them feel less detached from the world. On top of this, they can help them think logically and observe society objectively. The challenges that individualists face with type five are overdramatizing their self-image in a negative way, struggling to connect with other people, and becoming more withdrawn from society so they can hide their emotions easier (Cloete, n.d.).

Center Points

Individualists are part of the heart center. If you have a type four personality, you want to know why you are different from other people (Cloete, n.d.). You are proud of your individuality, which can be both a strength and weakness towards your character. Furthermore, type fours tend to internalize their shame, which is often how they begin to create their unique character.

Type four's strengths:

- Compassion
- Feeling deeply
- Empathy
- Creative
- Idealistic

Type four's weaknesses:

- Overly sensitive
- Dissatisfaction
- Demanding
- Self-absorbed
- Withdrawn
- Moody

How to Grow Personally

Keep Your Thoughts Positive

Keeping your thoughts positive will help you stay in the right mindset and avoid lengthy negative conversations with your imagination. Once you are able to accomplish this, you will begin to increase your self-esteem and confidence. Over time, you will find that you are able to turn negative life experiences into more positive experiences, which will help you grow and learn as an individualist.

One of the facts about being a type four personality, is you might never feel like you've found your true place in this world. You will often feel, whether you admit it to yourself or not, that you are unique and hold special characteristics unlike many other people. When you start to feel this way, you have to remember to maintain a positive mindset. You need to realize that the best thing you can do is remain unique but not allow yourself to become too withdrawn from society (Cloete, n.d.).

Use Self-Discipline to Help Manage Your Emotions

When you use self-discipline in your daily life, you will find that you start to feel less stressed and are able to manage your emotions better. It is important to know that self-discipline can show itself in many forms, from following a daily schedule to make sure you take time to meditate or any other way to release your negative emotions. For example, you will want to get enough sleep so that you will be better able to manage your emotions and struggles of being highly sensitive and individualistic. Furthermore, making sure that you find time for yourself so you can release any negativity will help you gain better control over transforming your negative thoughts into positive ones (Cloete, n.d.).

Don't Procrastinate

Another helpful way to grow your personality is to not procrastinate. Part of this you will learn through self-discipline. The other part you will learn as you stop procrastinating. Individualists will often put off tasks until they feel ready to do them. This happens because they feel like they have to prepare themselves in order to take on what they need to accomplish. However, there is never truly a correct time to do everything, especially if you are not looking forward to what you are doing.

Procrastination can make your emotions stronger, especially when it comes to negative emotions, such as stress. Therefore, once you stop procrastinating and start working on your tasks when you need to, you will find you are more capable of handling your emotions. Furthermore, you will start to gain self-confidence and believe that your self-image is more positive overall. Procrastination can interfere with a positive mindset, therefore, you want to do what you can to work on your tasks as soon as possible (Cloete, n.d.).

Chapter 6
The Investigator

The investigator's growth line runs from point five to point eight while its stress line runs from point five to point seven. The primary words used to describe the investigator, who is also referred to as the observer and the specialist, are innovative, isolated, perceptive, and secretive. Some popular investigator personalities are Siddhartha Gautama Buddha, Stephen Hawking, Vincent van Gogh, Tim Burton, and Kurt Cobain ("Type Five," n.d.).

What is the Investigator?

The biggest desire of a type five personality is to be knowledgeable and skillful. The biggest fear for an investigator is to be perceived as useless and incapable. Investigators are able to focus on very detailed and complicated tasks and tend to be insightful. They are also very curious and can become preoccupied by their thoughts and the situations around them. The biggest motivators for a type five personality are learning, being able to defend themselves from society with their knowledge, and being able to understand the environment and people around them ("Type Five," n.d.).

Investigators are the personality type who want to find out the truth. They not only want to learn the truth, but they want to know the in-depth version of the truth. They want to know every detail, why something happened, when it happened, and how it happened. Unfortunately, this can also cause investigators to think that they can never fully function in today's society. In fact, they can become more withdrawn because they are afraid of what is going to happen ("Type Five," n.d.).

Of course, this feeling is only escalated because type five personalities believe they can't accomplish tasks like other people can. They don't often possess the strong self-confidence that most other personalities do, which can often hold them back from becoming successful.

For investigators to fully understand why something is happening, they have to be able to observe it. They will then take the time they need to understand what they saw, heard, and why it happened. They are critical thinkers and will take the time they need in order to reach a conclusion. Of course, this can cause issues when it comes to deadlines and communicating with other people. This can often make people think that investigators procrastinate. However, they don't often procrastinate like most other personalities do. Instead, they are just taking their time so they can learn what happened and reach their own conclusion ("Type Five," n.d.).

Because of their observation and critical thinking skills, type five personalities are often creating and inventing new things. Because they want to see how things work, they are able to take something apart, put it back together, or create something new. These skills make investigators feel confident as they start to believe they can make their own place in this world. At the same time, their need to observe, learn, and create can often cause them to become more withdrawn from society. While they are fine with having a select group of friends, they do tend to feel lonely ("Type Five," n.d).

One of the biggest struggles for investigators is they don't like to face their problems head on. Because of this, they often have trouble forming relationships and in general struggle with functioning in society, especially within groups of people. In fact, one of the biggest obstacles investigators can face is having to accomplish a task in a team. They are much better at performing tasks individually ("Type Five," n.d.).

Levels of Integration

Healthy Levels

The healthiest level for an investigator is level one. Type five personalities who reach this level are open-minded. They also tend to be pioneer investigators. They will often spend their time figuring out new ways to accomplish tasks.

A level two can gain a lot of insight through everything they experience in their life. They have a strong ability to concentrate on tasks but can become too drawn into the task and can cause them to lose sight of what they needed to originally do. They are very observant, mentally alert, and good at predicting what will happen in the future because of their observational skills (Cloete, n.d.).

A level three will always look for something new to learn. They will often become an expert in their field of study, are highly independent, and skillful masters (Cloete, n.d.).

Average Levels

An investigator at a level four will often try to find new ways to do something. They will view things as a challenge, which will in turn help them to absorb the information they want to learn. They are often busy gathering as many resources as they can, so they can increase their knowledge. It is around this level where the investigator starts to become in-tune with their skills and works on ways to master their talents (Cloete, n.d.).

A level five will start to fall victim to their fantasy world. While they remain curious and continue to expand their knowledge, they also become detached from the things they learn and the ideas this knowledge puts into their head. It's during this phase that they start to focus more on dark topics, which can contribute to their increasingly morbid thoughts as they get trapped within their mind (Cloete, n.d.).

An investigator at level six is deemed argumentative and pessimistic. While they continue to learn, they don't focus on growing their knowledge like investigators do in the healthy level or the higher average levels. A type five personality would rather not have people interfere with their thoughts and tend to withdraw from society (Cloete, n.d.).

Unhealthy Levels

A level seven investigator is not only aggressive but highly unstable. They are victims of their dark thoughts, which often leads them to become repelled by other people. As a result, they become increasingly isolated from society (Cloete, n.d.).

An investigator who is at a level eight starts to become horrified by their increasingly dark thoughts. While they continue to dive into these thoughts, they become frightened by them and often realize that they are unhealthy. However, most do their best not to focus on how shockingly horrible their thoughts are as they become progressively obsessed with them (Cloete, n.d.).

The unhealthiest level for an investigator is a level nine. At this point, a type five personality will often suffer a psychotic break. They are often diagnosed with various mental disorders such as schizophrenia (Cloete, n.d.).

Subtypes of the Investigator

Social Category is Totem

One reason a type five personality is called the investigator is that they often carry characteristics that are associated with investigators. People who fit this personality type tend to look into the details of situations around them. They want to know why something happens and how it happened. They will often do their own research or talk to people in order to find out what is going on. They don't tend to listen to what other people say, partially because they are also known to disconnect themselves from other people. By disconnecting themselves, they are able to better manage their emotions and thoughts, which can help them have a clear mind when they are learning (Cloete, n.d.).

Self-Preservation Category is Castle

Investigators are believed to be introverts because they tend to withdraw from society. They keep close to a small number of friends, and they like to remain in their home as this helps keep their social boundaries clear. At the same time, they can often be seen observing people and situations as they try to figure out what is going on around them and why. Their need to be left alone in their home can often create a negative effect because they can find themselves protecting their privacy at an intense degree, which makes it hard for them to let their guard down if they need help from others or if people want to socialize with them (Cloete, n.d.).

One-on-One Category is Confident

Investigators will feel a lot of compassion and become very passionate towards a couple of people in their private life. However, this can help them to thrive socially, or it can cause them to test their partner or friends to make sure that they will not be harmed or betrayed by them. A type five personality might test their partner because they are afraid of letting their guard down. At the same time, investigators can become overly protective of their partner because they don't want to share this person with anyone else (Cloete, n.d.).

Relationships with Other Types

Like with the other personalities, investigators can get along with any type of personality. However, they are more compatible with type three personalities and less compatible with type two. Any personality that a type five gets to know can help them thrive or in other cases, cause more struggles. However, because a type five is typically non-confrontational, they won't often express how they feel. Instead, they will start to withdraw from people and society as a whole ("Relationships (Type Combinations)," n.d.).

Wing Types

One wing type for the investigator is a type four, also known as the individualist. Type four can help type five find a balance within their life, especially when it relates to how passionate they become about certain people. Other strengths include connecting with others, learning how to connect their emotions to their thoughts, and connecting themselves to their intuitions. The challenges that the investigator faces due to this wing type include becoming attached to fantasies, becoming depressed because they feel misunderstood by society, and withdrawing further away from society to avoid confrontation (Cloete, n.d.).

The second wing type for the investigator is a type six personality. The strengths that type six brings to type five include being able to understand someone else's point of view, increasing their connection with groups of people, and increasing their self-confidence so they become more comfortable in social settings. The challenges that a type five may experience from a type six are becoming more socially withdrawn because they believe they can't trust people and think that they will upset people if they continue to be overly social (Cloete, n.d.).

Center Points

If you have a type five personality, you are a part of the head center (Cloete, n.d.). You think that you have to know everything about the situation before walking into it. Therefore, you will often observe everything about what is going on, so that you know exactly what to expect.

Type five's strengths:

- Intellectual
- Dependable
- Self-reliant

- Calm
- Thoughtful
- Respectful

Type five's weaknesses:

- Overthinking
- Hoarding
- Isolation
- Detached

How to Grow Personally

Learn to Relax

Investigators often struggle with learning to relax. This can make them more intense, which can cause them to withdraw from people because they don't want to cause any problems, especially since they also don't like confrontation. Therefore, type five personalities need to take extra care to make sure they are able to unwind and find something, such as a hobby, that will help them relieve some of the stressors in their life. For example, going out for a walk, riding a bicycle, or joining a gym are great ways to relieve stress. However, some investigators are highly creative, which means that they might be able to relieve their stress through art or writing (Cloete, n.d.).

Avoid Distractions

Type five personalities are curious about everything, which can cause them to be easily distracted. When this happens, they often forget about the tasks they have to accomplish or else fall behind on them, which leads to the need of an extension on their deadlines or pushing the work aside. Therefore, it is important to make sure you accomplish your tasks, even if it means you need to use self-discipline or find techniques that will help you stop from getting too distracted by situations that aren't as important (Cloete, n.d.).

Don't Get Trapped by Your Thoughts

Because investigators are always thinking and trying to learn new things, they can easily become trapped in their own thoughts. When this happens, they tend to avoid the people around them and further withdraw from society. Because this can make an investigator feel lonely over time, often leading them to depression, it is important to make sure that they schedule social time into their calendar. Even if you only have a few friends, which many personalities are comfortable with, you will still want to make time to go to the movies, go out to eat, or hang out with them and play video games at home. This will help you keep a balance in your life so you don't feel trapped by your thoughts (Cloete, n.d.).

Chapter 7
The Loyalist

The stress line for the sixth personality type, the loyalist, heads to line three. The growth line goes from point six to point nine. The primary words used to describe a loyalist are responsible, suspicious, engaging, and anxious. Some famous people who exhibit a loyalist personality are Prince Harry, Mel Gibson. Mark Wahlberg, Julia Roberts, Mark Twain, Malcolm X, and Robert F. Kennedy ("Type Six," n.d).

What is the Loyalist?

Those with a type six personality are known to be excellent troubleshooters. Typically, they are able to problem-solve quickly and are considered to be hard-working, dependent, and trustworthy. Some of their motivations include support from other people, security, and being able to fight off their fears and anxiety. Because loyalists can often foresee the future, they become defensive and cautious of situations that can create undesirable results ("Type Six," n.d.).

The basic desire for a loyalist is to feel secure and have support from the people surrounding them. The biggest fear of a loyalist is losing the guidance and support they have from people closest to them. Out of all nine personality types in the Enneagram theory, they are known to be the most loyal to their close friends and family. In fact, they can become just as loyal to their thoughts and beliefs as well. However, if they reach an unhealthy level, they can become withdrawn, aggressive, and exhibit signs of paranoia ("Type Six," n.d.).

One downside to a type six personality is they tend to lack self-confidence. This is why they often seek guidance and approval from other people. They think that they are not able to perform tasks which other people can. If they can't find someone that can guide them to reach a healthy balance, they will be their own guidance through the use of their imagination and what they believe is right ("Type Six," n.d.).

Loyalists are part of the thinking center, which means that they are constantly thinking. At the same time, they are easily afraid of their own thoughts. This often occurs because they have an internal fear that they are going to be wrong and cause problems for other people. This is why they are known to have high levels of anxiety.

It is often due to the anxiety a loyalist feels that will lead them to an unhealthy level of integration. Loyalists are often aware of their anxiety, therefore, they do what they can to try to combat their thoughts ("Type Six," n.d.). If they are successful, they are more likely to follow a healthy level of integration. However, if they are not successful, they will be more likely to fall victim to an unhealthy level of integration.

Because their anxiety is so strong, they will often spend time looking for the reasons that are causing their anxiety. Sometimes, they will realize there is no reason for their anxious behavior over something minor.

The biggest challenge that a type six personality faces is trying to build their safety net, so they can do their best to remain at a healthy level of integration ("Type Six," n.d.). They also want to build this form of security, so that they can protect themselves against their anxiety, thoughts, and emotions. They believe that if they are able to build a safety net, they will be able to deal with the stresses of life.

Levels of Integration

Healthy Level

Loyalists at the healthiest level, meaning level one, are some of the most positive thinkers. They have full trust in their feelings and beliefs, and are known to be independent. They have courage, are very trusting of other people, and believe in true equality (Cloete, n.d.).

At level two, a loyalist believes that trust is important and that most people can be trusted. They are known to have very strong relationships with others and feel deeply (Cloete, n.d.).

A loyalist who is at a level three is hard-working, trustworthy, responsible, and have a strong sense of community involvement. They often dedicate themselves to social movements which they strongly believe in. They believe that the world can become a secure place for everyone and are willing to sacrifice themselves in order to make this happen (Cloete, n.d.).

Average Level

A loyalist who is at a level four enjoy schedules, organization, and structure. They will spend the majority of their time trying to improve environmental conditions for other people, however, they won't always think their actions through. Their main focus is to make everything and everyone safe and secure (Cloete, n.d.).

A level five loyalist starts to become passive-aggressive when they think that people are taking advantage of them or asking them to take on too much. They experience an internal confusion on how to better themselves and their negative thought patterns, which can cause them to become angry and annoyed at other people (Cloete, n.d.).

A loyalist who is at a level six will often blame other people for their problems and become very insecure about the person they are. They are highly suspicious of other people because they believe that people cannot be trusted. They are known to be sarcastic, defensive, and argumentative. As a result, many loyalists tend to withdraw from society (Cloete, n.d.).

Unhealthy Level

A loyalist who is at a level seven will become very unstable and defenseless. They will look for an authoritative figure who can teach them how to defend themselves and, when they find one, they tend to become very dependent on this authoritative figure. However, they tend to struggle with relationships, which often drives them further into isolation. Loyalists at this level can become increasingly lonely (Cloete, n.d.).

Loyalists who are at a level eight tend to become paranoid. They think that people are out to get them and that no one can be trusted. They often turn to violence when they feel fear (Cloete, n.d.).

A loyalist who is at a level nine is often classified as someone with avoidant personality disorder or paranoid personality disorder. They often turn to thoughts of suicide because they want to escape their thoughts of paranoia and self-destructive behavior (Cloete, n.d.).

Subtypes of the Loyalist

Social Category is Duty

Type six personalities who are part of this subcategory are often compared to type one personalities. This is because they both share similar characteristics. Loyalists will do what they can to help those who they believe are weaker than them. They are also strict on making sure they follow rules and guidelines. They are known to be hard-workers and will do whatever they can to make sure they succeed in the tasks they are assigned (Cloete, n.d.).

Self-Preservation Category is Warmth

Loyalists are often afraid of making a mistake, which is why they don't share their ideas or opinions. They are known to be caring and warm individuals who tend to get along with any type of personality. In fact, they often spend their time with people because they enjoy the company of others. At the same time, they can have an internal fear about people noticing their insecurities (Cloete, n.d.).

One-on-One Category is Intimidation

This subtype is the countertype of the loyalist. They are often bold and typically aren't afraid to take the steps they need to take in order to defend themselves. They are known to be emotionally and mentally strong individuals that may run towards danger instead of away from it, no matter how much fear they feel. Loyalists under this subtype can be viewed as intimidating (Cloete, n.d.).

Relationships with Other Types

Type six personalities tend to become a strong friend or partner for any personality type. While they tend to become fast friends with personalities nine, two, three, and four, they can still face struggles with these types of personalities. Of course, a type six personality is also able to mix well with another type six personality. However, they will often find themselves trying to avoid confrontation because they share a lot of the same characteristics ("Relationships (Type Combinations)," n.d.).

Wing Types

One wing type for the loyalist is a type five personality. The strengths which the investigator brings to the loyalist are opening them up to being more accepting of other viewpoints, keeping their fears in check through analysis, allowing them to trust their internal validations, and feeling more confident in themselves. The challenges loyalists face with investigators include increasing their anxiety levels and avoiding confrontation (Cloete, n.d.).

Another wing type for the loyalist is a type seven personality. The strengths that this personality brings to the loyalist includes trusting other people, being optimistic, and feeling comfortable within society. The weaknesses that type seven brings to a type six personality are giving them ideas on how to escape situations so they can avoid confrontation and a fear of pain along with anxiety over trivial matters (Cloete, n.d.).

Center Points

If you have a type six personality, you are part of the head center and more likely to think of the worst possible outcome when faced with a danger (Cloete, n.d.). This is your natural reaction to danger because you believe it will help you prepare for what can possibly happen. While you generally look to authoritative figures for guidance, you will also rebel against them because you believe they become too attached and you want more independence from them.

Type six's strengths:

- Critical-thinking
- Strategizing
- Bravery
- Sensitivity
- Humor
- Loyalty

Type six's weaknesses:

- Overly energetic
- Anxiety
- Pessimism
- Hyper-vigilant

How to Grow Personally

Understand Anxiety is Normal

Many people in the world experience anxiety. In fact, anxiety is a part of all nine personality types in the Enneagram theory.

Once a loyalist remembers that they are not different from the other personality types because of their anxiety, they are better able to deal with the stresses of life. Loyalists often think that they are the only ones who deal with anxiety, even though everyone experiences different types of anxiety. Some people experience anxiety over trivial situations and thoughts. Worry is part of everyone's daily life. On top of this, everyone is able to learn techniques to help them deal with their insecurities and anxious thoughts (Cloete, n.d.).

Learn What Your Stressors Are

Stress and anxiety go hand in hand. Therefore, when you are able to identify what your stressors are, you will be able to learn how to manage them accordingly. You learn to control your anxiety and your anxious thoughts (Cloete, n.d.).

Become More Trusting and Self-Confident

When a loyalist is at a healthy level, they are very trusting and self-confident. Every loyalist can reach this level and one way to do so is by learning to trust other people. Type six personalities need to learn that they can trust that others think they are generally good people. They need to believe themselves that people don't think of them in a negative way and that this is just a part of their anxiety and anxious thinking. If they are able to shift their mindset to this, they will become more trusting and self-confident (Cloete, n.d.).

Chapter 8
The Enthusiast

The stress line for the enthusiast runs from point seven to point two while the growth line runs from point seven to point five. The primary words used to describe a type eight personality are acquisitive, spontaneous, scattered, and versatile. Well-known people who are considered enthusiasts are Thomas Jefferson, Amelia Earhart, Robert Downey, Jr., Charlie Sheen, Paris Hilton, and Larry King ("Type Seven," n.d).

What is the Enthusiast?

Some of the main motivators for the enthusiast are freedom, keeping themselves occupied, happy, and avoiding pain. Their main fear is being in pain while their main desire is to know their needs are fulfilled. Type seven personalities are known to be very high-spirited, playful, have many talents, optimistic, and undisciplined. While they are always looking for something new to do as they enjoy seeking new and exciting adventures, they can also become easily exhausted from their adventures ("Type Seven," n.d.).

They are very curious about life and tend to look at the world with big and exciting eyes. In fact, many people would say they are similar to a kid in a candy shop. While they are very cheerful, they can also be domineering ("Type Seven," n.d.).

While they are at the head or thinking center, this doesn't necessarily mean that they think things through before making decisions. In fact, they can be very impulsive. At the same time, they are able to focus on their thoughts and are very practical.

In fact, some people often say that enthusiasts have two personalities that can switch in an instant ("Type Seven," n.d.). For example, they can go from being very playful and impulsive to behaving in an adult-like way and think thoroughly before they act or speak.

Type seven personalities love to learn and will often spend their time looking for new information to take in. Therefore, they are known to be quick learners. Because of this, they are also able to pick up new skills ("Type Seven," n.d.). They tend to value their skills, which can also cause conflict as they struggle to determine what career path to take in their lives.

Enthusiasts are often out of touch with their thinking center, which is what causes them to sometimes become impulsive ("Type Seven," n.d.). This can also cause problems for people who are trying to guide them into a healthy direction of integration. In return, a type seven personality can experience feelings of anxiety. When they start to feel anxious, they will cope with it by becoming busy with something. At the same time, they can sometimes struggle with making the right choices.

Levels of Integration

Healthy Level

Enthusiasts at a level one are often in awe of the world around them. They are highly grateful for what they have in life and believe that people act with the best intentions. They believe that people want to work together to make the world a better place. They also believe that we are continuously succeeding in this effort (Cloete, n.d.).

A level two enthusiast is very spontaneous and is considered an extrovert. Like the first level, they believe that people share a common good and are very enthusiastic about where the world is going. They believe that we will make the world a better place, especially if we continue to work together (Cloete, n.d.).

An enthusiast who is at a level three tends to focus on certain areas of their community when trying to do the best for others. They are very realistic about their goals and are known to be high achievers (Cloete, n.d.).

Average Level

An enthusiast at a level four is more focused on money and trends than trying to make the world a better place. They aren't happy with the choices that life has given them and often look for better experiences (Cloete, n.d.).

A level five enthusiast has a fear of becoming bored with tasks and the people around them. Therefore, they are known to be very outgoing and loud. On top of this, they are known to be hyperactive. They make good performers. Furthermore, they often have trouble knowing what they need and what they want (Cloete, n.d.).

An enthusiast who is at a level six is very materialistic, greedy, and self-centered. This can make them very demanding as they often think they never have enough. For example, they more money they make, the more money they want to receive the next time. They are never truly grateful for what they have in life (Cloete, n.d.).

Unhealthy Level

An enthusiast who is at a level seven can become abusive and aggressive. They can often become addicted to drugs and alcohol and have trouble knowing when to stop, especially when they know they want something. They tend to have a lot of problems with money because they don't know how to manage their money (Cloete, n.d.).

An enthusiast who is at a level eight cannot control their impulses. At this point, their anxiety can reach a whole new high as they start to realize they can't control themselves. They also start to act out due to their impulses and frustrations when they can't get something they want (Cloete, n.d.).

A level nine enthusiast is often diagnosed with bipolar disorder as they go fluctuate between severe highs and severe lows. They have trouble coping because they realize they cannot manage their stresses and impulses. It is often at this stage that many enthusiasts start to contemplate suicide (Cloete, n.d.).

Subtypes of the Enthusiast

Social Category is Sacrifice

The sacrifice is the countertype for the enthusiast. This subtype will often sacrifice their needs in order to make the world a better place, especially for the people they love and support. At the same time, they want to become noticed for their sacrifices, thereby causing them to become judgmental of others if they are not recognized for their efforts (Cloete, n.d.).

Self-Preservation Category is Network

A type seven personality is typically considered extroverted as they enjoy hanging out with people, especially their close friends and family. They know how to help people and are often willing to do so, especially if it will bring more fun into their group. However, they might find themselves becoming too involved in pleasing others as this can become a motivator for them, which can send them into an unhealthy level of integration (Cloete, n.d.).

One-on-One Category is Fascination

Enthusiasts are known for their optimism and enthusiastic nature, which is how they received their name. However, they can become overly obsessed with the fantasy of making sure the world becomes a better place that they tend to forget about reality. When they see what the world is really like, they start to see the world as a gray place. This can often cause them to believe that the people they hang out with are boring and unwilling to help them turn the world into a more colorful and happier place (Cloete, n.d.).

Relationships with Other Types

While a type seven personality can get along with any other personality type, they mainly form relationships with types two, three, seven, and nine. In fact, they get along best with type nine personalities. Of course, as it is with any personality type, there are strengths and weaknesses brought on by these relationships ("Relationships (Type Combinations)," n.d.).

Wing Types

One of the wing types for a type seven personality is a type six, otherwise known as the loyalist. Like with any wing, the loyalist can bring about strengths and challenges into their relationship. The strengths that a type six can bring into the lives of a type seven includes commitment and a deeper understanding of their actions, mindfulness, and the act of taking things more seriously. The challenges that the loyalist brings to the enthusiast includes exaggeration of their fears, feeling like responsibilities are a burden, self-doubt, and the feeling of being irresponsible (Cloete, n.d.).

The second wing type for the enthusiast is a type eight personality. The strengths that the type eight brings with them includes assertiveness, learning how to plan better, becoming less afraid of feeling hurt, and learning to be honest with themselves and others. The challenges that type eight brings to an enthusiast are turning their assertiveness into aggression, wanting immediate satisfaction, and becoming self-absorbed (Cloete, n.d.).

Center Types

If you have a type seven personality, you are part of the head center and will try to turn your uncomfortable, fearful situations into something that is more exciting and comfortable (Cloete, n.d.). This occurs because people who are a type seven have a fear about becoming trapped in fearful situations. Therefore, they will do what they can in order to make themselves feel less fear.

Type seven's strengths:

- Energetic
- Quick-thinker
- Strong imagination
- Playful
- Optimistic

Type seven's weaknesses:

- Impatient
- Self-absorbed
- Unrealistic
- Isolation
- Uncommitted

How to Grow Personally

Control Your Impulses

Once you learn to control your impulses, you will be able to make better decisions and realize that you can't have everything exactly the way you want it and when you want it. Once you come to this realization, you will be able to judge whether you really need something, or you just want something. On top of this, you will get a better sense of what is good for you and what isn't (Cloete, n.d.).

Listen to People

When you start listening to other people, you will start to learn more than you ever thought possible. You will start to make better decisions because you will believe that others want the best for you and, therefore, won't send you down an unhealthy path. You will also learn that other people can be very interesting, and that they can help you become a better person. Furthermore, you will learn to enjoy your time alone because the more you connect with people, the more you will realize that you need your solitude to help you remain relaxed (Cloete, n.d.).

Chapter 9
The Protector

A type eight personality is called the protector, otherwise known as the controller. This is because while they also focus on protecting their environment, they also want to remain in control of everything and everyone around them. However, another name for the protector is the challenger. The stress line for the protector runs from point eight to point five and the growth line from point eight to point two. A few of the most common terms used to describe the type eight personality are decisive, confrontational, self-confident, and willful. Some of the most well-known people who follow in the path of the protector are John Wayne, Bette Davis, Roseanne Barr, Aretha Franklin, and Martin Luther King, Jr. ("Type Eight," n.d).

What is the Protector?

The protector is known to be strong, self-confident, protective, resourceful, and assertive. At the same time, they can also become domineering and feel the need to control everything around them. The main desire of a type is to be able to protect themselves. Their fear is being controlled by other people or being harmed by someone. The same way they want to protect their environment and others, they also want to be able to protect themselves ("Type Eight," n.d).

Some of the main motivations for type eight personalities are being able to resist their weaknesses, showing their strengths, being able to control their environment, and becoming self-reliant (Type Eight,"n.d).

One of the biggest reasons why the protector is often referred to as the challenger is because this type of personality is the one that is most likely to challenge themselves and other people ("Type Eight," n.d). In fact, they like to see how far they can go and in turn become self-confident when they see they are succeeding in tasks they deem challenging.

Type eight personalities are often referred to as protectors because they have to control their environment. While some people might see this as domineering, type eight personalities do this in order to protect everything around them, including themselves and other people. Protectors feel the need to have complete control of the environment so they can protect everyone, including themselves ("Type Eight," n.d).

A type eight's biggest fear is harm, however, there is another part to this fear. Not only does this include harm to themselves, but it also includes harm to other people and their environment. From a young age, protectors realize that they will have to be persistent and strong if they want to become the protectors they believe they need to be. This is because they know they will need to do their best to make sure no harm comes to themselves or others. Therefore, while their biggest fear is harm on others and the environment, they are more likely to fear loss of control than actual harm. This is because they realize they have to keep control in order so that they, others, and their environment may remain unharmed ("Type Eight," n.d).

Even though they are afraid of being harmed, they can usually take on a lot of physical harm. This is because they are known to be emotionally, mentally, and physically tough. However, they can handle physical harm a lot better than emotional and mental harm. In fact, they would rather be harmed physically. This is because they hold their health at a very high standard and often take it for granted ("Type Eight," n.d). Of course, this can cause issues with other personalities because type eight personalities are less likely to take care of their overall health and instead care for the well-being of other people.

Type eight personalities focus on protecting their environment. While the protector believes he or she is doing the right thing, people will think otherwise. This can throw the protector off-guard and wonder why people think otherwise when he or she works so hard to make sure that everyone is taken care of and protected. When this happens, they tend to become emotionally distant from the people closest to them. Unfortunately, when a type eight feels this way, he or she will also distance themselves from the rest of society ("Type Eight," n.d). This happens because the protector feels misunderstood and rejected, which in turn is a form of emotional harm.

Levels of Integration

Healthy Level

Protectors at a level one are their own masters. They are self-restrained, courageous, and willing to put themselves in physical harm in order to get what they want. Protectors at this level are often seen as heroes as they are constantly working towards protecting their environment and others over themselves (Cloete, n.d.).

Type eight personalities who are at a level two are known to be very strong and self-confident. They know what they want and what they need, and can become very assertive when it comes time to take action. They have an attitude of knowing that they can truly take over the world (Cloete, n.d.).

Protectors at a level three are natural-born leaders. People tend to look up to them as they are very authoritative and commanding. They do what they have to do to make sure that action takes place. In general, this level of type eight personalities are seen as very caring, strong, protective, great providers, and honorable (Cloete, n.d.).

Average Level

Protectors at a level four have a strong need for financial independence. They know what resources they need in order to gain this independence and are not afraid to become risk-takers or work hard in order to achieve it. While they can be seen as protective towards others, their main aim is to get what they want. They don't often ignore their own needs in order to help others; they ignore their own needs in order to reach the financial independence they want (Cloete, n.d.).

A level five type eight personality not only focuses on dominating their environment but also other people. Instead of seeing this as a form of protection, many people start to see this as a form of control. This is because they have a very boss-like demeanor and can become very forceful. At this level, protectors will start to believe that people aren't treating them with respect they deserve, therefore, they are not considered as equals (Cloete, n.d.).

Protectors who are at a level six are known to be extremely intimidating. In fact, at this level, people with other types of personalities start to become afraid of what they are capable of.

They can become very confrontational and loud in order to get what they want. They do not like to back down and will continue to use threats in order to get other people to listen to them (Cloete, n.d.).

Unhealthy Level

Protectors who are at a level seven are at one of the highest unhealthiest levels. At this point, they become completely dictatorial in order to get people to listen to them and have control over them. While other personalities will start to band against them, they will become ruthless and make sure that they stay on top. Protectors at this level are known to be violent criminals and con-artists (Cloete, n.d.).

Protectors who are at a level eight often develop delusional thoughts about the power they hold. They believe they are untouchable (Cloete, n.d.).

Type eight personalities who are at a level nine are known to have sociopathic tendencies. They will destroy everything and anyone in their path if they feel threatened. In fact, they would rather destroy themselves than have to surrender to anyone else. Protectors at this level are barbaric and often show symptoms of antisocial personality disorder (Cloete, n.d.).

Subtypes of the Protector

Social Category is Solidarity

Solidarity is seen as the countertype for a type eight personality. Protectors in this group will often be viewed more as a type two than a type eight. This is because they tend to focus more on helping others, which makes them push aside their needs and wants. Protectors under this subtype have a strong sense to help the world socially by focusing on social issues that they think are important. They don't like to see injustice and they are very sensitive when it comes to the needs of other people. At the same time, they will become a shield for anyone they think is facing some form of injustice (Cloete, n.d.).

Self-Preservation Category is Satisfaction

Many people can view the protector of this subtype to have two distinct personalities. First, people will see this person to be very caring and generous. They typically take on a very comforting nature and can become a guardian or role model to many people as they take on the role of a mother, father, aunt, uncle, or sibling. In this role, type eight personalities will do whatever they can to help the people who need their help. However, they also believe that they should be able to get just as much in return. This is when people see a different side to this subtype as they can become aggressive and manipulative when they want something. While they will make sure everyone else's needs are satisfied, they will make sure their own needs are satisfied as well (Cloete, n.d.).

One-on-One Category is Possession

Type eight personalities who are a part of this subtype will be viewed as leaders and rebels. They will do whatever they need to do to make sure they reach the top and get to where they want to be. This subtype can easily be mistaken for a type four personality because they can become very impulsive when they want something. However, they do not have the characteristics of a type four personality. They are, in fact, acting this way because they become unapologetic when they want to reach a goal (Cloete, n.d.).

Relationships with Other Types

Like with the other personality types, type eight personalities tend to get along with other type eight's ("Relationships (Type Combinations)," n.d.). The relationship will progress if all the personality types are at a healthier level of integration, rather than an unhealthy level. However, this doesn't mean that the protector will not experience conflict when it comes to other personality types. For example, a relationship with a type three personality can also become too much of a good thing for the protector. Because they are both very positive when at a healthy level of integration, they will ignore the challenges they face together. This means they tend to avoid confronting each other when there are disagreements. Instead, they will keep their conflicts bottled inside and continue to work with each other. This can cause them to grow increasingly hostile towards each other.

Wing Center

One wing for the protector is a type seven. The strengths that this personality type brings to a type eight includes a balance with planning and perspective, happiness, the realization that they do not have to complete tasks alone, and knowing the value in expressing their thoughts and emotions. The challenges that a type eight may face are an increase in their addictive personality, the need to fulfill their desires, and become increasingly self-absorbed. They will also focus less on the consequences of their actions (Cloete, n.d.).

The second wing for a type eight is a type nine. This wing can bring many strengths and challenges to the protector. Some of the strengths are the realization that the protector does not need to make something happen if it can occur naturally, a sense of balance in life, and becoming more laid back and calm. The challenges include neglecting themselves, becoming out of touch with themselves, and withdrawing from society. When the protector begins to withdraw from those around them, they will feel guilty and will harshly judge themselves (Cloete, n.d).

Center Type

People who have a type eight personality are not only part of the body center but also tend to be known for their anger and temper issues (Cloete, n.d.). They externalize their anger, and are not afraid to show this emotion. However, they also want to protect themselves so they will often build guards as a means for protection. Most of the time, they will become angry because they think someone is being mistreated.

Type eight's strengths:

- Fairness
- Generosity
- Bravery
- Strength
- Honest
- Protective

Type eight's weaknesses:

- Forgetful
- Controlling

- Angry
- Lustful
- Afraid of showing vulnerability

How to Grow Personally

Use Your Power Wisely

One of the best ways to grow personally is to make sure that you use your power wisely. You have a strong sense of power and have the capability to do a lot of good with it, however, you have to know how to use it in order to not fall victim to an unhealthy level of integration. Unfortunately, when people hold a lot of power, it is natural for them to believe they want more of this power. However, if you act with self-restraint, you will understand that your power is used to help and uplift people instead of controlling them and the environment.

You are very helpful when it comes to dealing with a crisis. With your power, you are able to maintain a calm mind and make people feel more at ease when times are tough. This is a very special trait to have since you are the only personality which really holds this type of power. Therefore, it is important to make sure to use your power wisely and with good intentions (Cloete, n.d.).

Keep Your Ego in Check

Most personalities will struggle with their ego, regardless of if it's expressed externally or internally. As a protector, you often use your ego to protect yourself. Therefore, when your ego starts to build up, you will start to believe that you have to protect yourself more from other people and factors within the environment. When this happens, you will become more sensitive to any slight disrespect or to someone threatening your environment. This can cause you to act out, sometimes violently. In order to maintain a healthy level of integration, you will want to make sure your ego is kept in check so you don't start to overthink perceived threats (Cloete, n.d.).

Chapter 10
The Mediator

The type nine personality is called the mediator, or otherwise known as the peacemaker. This is because their primary descriptive words are agreeable, complacent, reassuring, and receptive. They are also known to be very easy-going, accepting, and trusting. Their stress line runs from point nine to point six and their growth line runs from point nine to point three. Some of the most well-known people who are known to be mediators are Queen Elizabeth II, John F. Kennedy, Jr., Abraham Lincoln, Janet Jackson, Jim Henson, and Walt Disney ("Type Nine," n.d).

What is the Mediator?

Some of the mediators' biggest motivators are bringing peace into their environment, being able to resist something that can disrupt them, and being able to avoid conflict. Their biggest desire is to have a peace of mind while their strongest fear is separation or loss. In a nutshell, they are known to be supportive, creative, and accepting. In fact, one of the biggest reasons they are often referred to as peacemakers over mediators is because they are the personality that will do everything in their power to bring peace into their environment and the lives of others ("Type Nine," n.d).

At the same time, type nine personalities will go above and beyond to ignore what is wrong in the world and with other people ("Type Nine," n.d). They don't like confrontation, therefore, they will use whatever means they can to bring peace into the situation and environment. If they are unable to bring peace into a situation, they will often react by becoming numb.

Mediators can also become out of touch with reality. When this happens, they often retreat to their mind and create a fantasy world, which allows them to continue to cope with what is going on around them, whether bad or good. This is when type nine personalities will start to use their personality powers against themselves ("Type Nine," n.d). They will feel so out of balance that they will start to struggle within their daily life.

However, when type nine personalities are able to remain balanced, they will be able to use their powers to help people in difficult situations. When they become in-tune with what they can do, they will use their energy to make peace with the situation. When they reach this level, they are able to critically think about the best way to solve the situation in a peaceful way rather than try to ignore the problem ("Type Nine," n.d). After all this, they will begin to think that if they cannot bring peace to the whole problem, then an issue still exists. Therefore, mediators think it is best to resolve the problem right away so that it doesn't come back a second time.

Mediators are also known to be one of the most spiritual personalities of the Enneagram theory. This is because they are known to be spiritual seekers, who not only want to form a strong internal connection with people but with their environment and the universe as a whole. In fact, while they are always working to keep peace among people, they are also working to create harmony within the world itself. Therefore, in order for them to truly believe they are fulfilling their work, they have to keep an open mind, focus on relaxation, let go of tension, stay away from mental, emotional, and physical pain, practice patience, and believe in unity over separation ("Type Nine," n.d).

Levels of Integration

Healthy Level

A mediator at a level one has a strong sense of fulfillment and is one with themselves. They are happiest with their lives, have great relationships with other people, and hold strong connections to their environment (Cloete, n.d.).

Type nine personalities which are at a level two are emotionally stable and calm. They are very trusting of other people, who also view mediators as very trustworthy. They are also known to be extremely patient, good-natured, and genuinely care about people and the environment. Many people believe they lead simple and innocent lives (Cloete, n.d.).

Mediators who are at a level three are extremely supportive and want the best for others. They are reassuring, optimistic, and tend to have a calming influence on other people. They are thought to be natural-born healers and are great at bringing people together for the common good. Furthermore, they are strong communicators and empathetic to others ("Type Nine," n.d.).

Average Level

Mediators who are at a level four often show more fear than mediators who are at a healthy level. They tend to be known as people pleasers because they will often go by what other people want, even if it's the opposite of what they want. This is because one of their biggest fears is conflict, which means they feel more comfortable going with the flow (Cloete, n.d.).

Type nine personalities at a level five start to walk away from the problems surrounding them. They don't want to disengage, but they would rather not deal with the conflict. They also believe that if they ignore the problem, it will go away on its own. They will start to tune people out, along with their environment, so that they don't have to focus on what they believe isn't right. As a result, they will start to create a fantasy world for themselves as they withdraw from society ("Type Nine," n.d.).

Mediators who are at a level six won't completely ignore problems but they will minimize them and try to bring a type of peace into their environment. Sometimes, they don't care at what price. They become stubborn and take on magical thinking to help them come up with solutions to their problems that will make people happy. However, other people see mediators at this level as uncaring, uninterested, and unresponsive (Cloete, n.d.).

Unhealthy Level

Mediators who are at a level seven think that they can't take on the problems they face. Therefore, they start to disconnect from their environment and society. Because of this, they neglect themselves and can become a danger to themselves or others ("Type Nine," n.d.).

Mediators who are at a level eight will do anything in their power to block out what they don't want to see or hear. At this point, they start to become numb about the world around them.

In fact, they can become so disconnected that they begin to struggle with daily functioning (Cloete, n.d.).

Type nine personalities at a level nine will create different types of personalities to help them cope with the stress they experience in their lives. This is commonly referred to as multiple personality disorder. They become disoriented and are not able to function in their day to day life ("Type Nine," n.d.).

Subtypes of the Mediator

Social Category is Participation

The mediator is known to be a social butterfly. They are typically very popular in their group setting because of their personality. As participants, they do whatever they can to make sure the people around them are happy, even if this means ignoring their own beliefs, stresses, and problems. They do this because they fear becoming a burden. Therefore, they often think it's best to deal with their problems themselves, or allow their closest friends and family to help them. While they don't like to burden others, a mediator at a healthy level will realize that he or she can't always deal with his or her problems alone and will ask for help when necessary. Participation is considered to be the countertype for the mediator (Cloete, n.d.).

Self-Preservation Category is Appetite

This type of mediator understands that they need to take care of themselves in the same way that they take care of others. Type nine personalities typically fall under this subtype when they also have a lot of type eight personality in them. They want to make sure people around them are happy and protected, including themselves. They have found, what they consider to be a healthy balance between taking care of other people, their surroundings, and themselves. They can quickly become upset when people come into their reality and try to ruin the balance they have created, which is usually when they start to form negative relationships with other personalities (Cloete, n.d.).

One-on-One Category is Fusion

This subtype of type nine personalities struggle to take care of themselves like they do other people. In fact, they believe by helping others, they are helping themselves. In ways, this does work because the mediators feel a sense of pride and comfort in their actions when they are helping other people. This help feeds their demands to take care of themselves. However, this can only work for some of their personal needs. Unfortunately, type nine personalities in this subtype tend to ignore or push away their issues or feelings about certain things because they want to focus more of their attention on others (Cloete, n.d.).

Relationships with Other Types

The mediator can have a healthy relationship with any other of the personality types. The mediator doesn't like confrontation, so this type of personality will often find techniques to avoid it. However, when they are faced with confrontation, they will try to do it in a way where they won't cause any emotional or physical harm to the other person. However, the way they go about doing this also depends on the mediator's level of integration ("Relationships (Type Combinations)," n.d.).

Wing Center

One wing for the mediator is the type one personality. The strengths that type one brings to the mediator includes giving them structure and focus over their perspectives, motivation to do what he or she needs to do, and offering support as the mediator works towards their goals. While mediators can take the time to make sure their tasks are completed, the support and help from type one is an important factor to help them achieve these tasks (Cloete, n.d.).

Another wing type for the mediator is type eight. This type will give the mediator strengths by not only helping them become more active but also giving them a sense of power. Furthermore, the protector will provide the mediator with a sense of balance, which will allow the mediator to flourish into a unique individual instead of being someone who follows the crowd. A type eight personality will also help the mediator become more confident and bold, which will allow them to protect themselves when they are feeling attacked (Cloete, n.d.).

Center Point

If you have a type nine personality, you are part of the body center and you will turn your anger into peace (Cloete, n.d.). This is why you are considered the peacemaker. You might find yourself simply ignoring things that make you angry because you do your best to maintain harmony for yourself and those around you.

Type nine's strengths:

- Non-judgmental
- Caring
- Approachable
- Supportive
- Great moderator
- Adaptive
- Caring

Type nine's weaknesses:

- Indecisive
- Forgetful
- Stubborn
- Avoidant

How to Grow Personally

Notice Your Emotions

It is important for the mediator to notice their emotions whether they are in a difficult situation or not. The more you realize that it is okay to have these emotions, the less likely you will try to disconnect from yourself, other people, and your environment. On top of this, you will be able to reach and remain at a healthy level of integration for your personality. This means that you will be able to face situations by thinking of the best ways to overcome negativity in a peaceful way and be able to continue your daily tasks to the best of your ability (Cloete, n.d.).

There is No Way to Avoid Conflict and Negativity

You also need to make sure that you are aware of what is going on around you. While you don't want to focus on negativity, it is a part of life. It will be part of your emotions, your environment, and the people around you. There is no way to completely avoid conflict and negativity. These are factors that will help you maintain a healthy level of integration if you learn to face them like you can anything else. This will become easier once you realize you have the power to do so. You have the power to change a negative situation into a positive one because of your peaceful nature. If you're wanting to withdraw from society because you're struggling, it is important to make sure you force yourself to continue on your path. In order to grow and improve your special personality, it's important to face your struggles, whether externally or internally. Doing this will help you become more mentally and emotionally engaged, which will only help you strengthen your powers (Cloete, n.d.).

Become Aware of Your Body

Not only do you want to become aware of your emotions, but you also need to become aware of your body and how you control your emotions. For example, if you start to exercise, you will increase your awareness of your body and how your body reacts to certain exercises. You want to become mindful of yourself. This will not only help you remain calm during a crisis, but it will also allow you to think more clearly and help you focus more on yourself, others, and the environment. You'll be able to see a problem coming before other people do, which means you will be able to bring peace to the situation before it escalates (Cloete, n.d.).

Examine How You Can Contribute to Problems

No one is perfect, no matter how hard you try to keep the peace. It is important for mediators to realize that they can make mistakes. For example, if you find yourself having issues with your spouse, you will want to take a step back and examine why these issues are occurring. You not only what to look at what you think your spouse is doing wrong but also how you contribute to the problem. Of course, this is not going to be easy, especially for a mediator. However, it is essential if you want to truly solve the problem in your peaceful ways (Cloete, n.d.).

Chapter 11
Testing

The only way you can truly find out what type of personality you have is to take the Enneagram test. This test is easy to find online or you can take it through a professional. You can find the Enneagram test at Eclectic Energies Enneagram Tests, which offers the test for free. You can also take the test at the Enneagram Institute.

About the Test

The Enneagram test will give you a series of questions and then tell you what personality you mainly fit into based on your answers. These are not complicated questions and focus solely on your personality. For example, the test might ask you if you consider yourself to be an overall happy person and then ask you to rate how happy or unhappy you are.

While there are many versions of the test, with a varying amount of questions, you are typically given pretty accurate results. The results will provide you with a list that shows you how influenced you are by each personality. You will also receive your main personality type, your second type, and so on. Therefore, you will also learn which personality type you are least likely to have.

However, this test will not just tell you what type of personality you have; it will also give you a detailed look at other parts of your personality, which you have already learned about in several chapters of this book. For example, you will learn about whether you are at a healthy, average, or unhealthy level of integration. You will also learn about your two wing centers, your center point, and your subtypes. At the same time, you will be able to get a sense of which personalities you relate to the most and which ones you will have more trouble getting along with.

Summary of the 9 Types and Their Subtypes

Because I have already discussed the nine personalities and their subtypes in detail, I won't focus heavily on them in this section. However, I also realize that you have been given a lot of information in this book, which can be overwhelming. Therefore, I did want to take time to give you a brief summary of the last nine chapters you just read.

The first personality type is known is the perfectionist. This is because they like to have everything in order and make sure to do their best at every task. The perfectionist's three subtypes are worry, zeal, and non-adaptability.

The second personality type is the helper. Because of their need to help others, this will be their main focus in life. However, this can also be a fault of theirs as they tend to forget about their own needs. Their three subtypes are ambition, privilege, and seduction.

The third personality is the achiever. People with this type of personality focus on becoming highly successful. Their three subtypes are prestige, security, and charisma.

The fourth personality is the individualist. This personality type is known to be highly sensitive and strives to make sure they are their unique self, even if they end up hiding it from a crowd. Their subtypes are shame, tenacity, and competition.

The fifth personality type is the investigator. They are known to pay close attention to detail. They want to know as much as they can about a situation and their environment and will spend a lot of time trying to figure things out. Their three subtypes are totem, castle, and confidence.

The sixth personality is the loyalist. They are given this name because they are loyal to others. Their main subtypes are duty, warmth, and intimidation.

The seventh personality is the enthusiast. They are known to be very outgoing and see the best in everyone and everything. They are very enthusiastic and optimistic. Their three subtypes are sacrifice, network, and fascination.

The eighth personality type is the protector and was given this name for a reason. They are known to be strong, resourceful, and are very protective of their environment. Their three subtypes are possession, solidarity, and satisfaction.

The ninth, and final, personality type is the mediator/peacemaker. This personality type is non-confrontational and will do whatever they can in order to maintain the peace around them. The three subtypes of the mediator include participation, appetite, and fusion.

Difference Between the Myers Briggs and the Enneagram

There are a lot of different personality tests that you can take. However, the Enneagram and the Myers-Briggs are two of the most common ones (Drenth, n.d.). This section will take a look at the differences between the two tests.

Nature vs. Nurture

One of the biggest differences between the two tests is that the Myers-Briggs tests focuses on nature whereas the Enneagram focuses on nurture (Drenth, n.d.). The Enneagram focuses more on the events that occur during your childhood. For instance, your childhood experiences, the good and the bad, will affect your personality when you reach adulthood. In fact, detailed reports of the personalities will often outline whether the problems you have in adulthood are a result of your mother or father.

The Myers-Briggs test looks at your personality type based on the moment you were born with it. While factors in your life can influence your personality, this test claims there are parts of your personality that have been a part of you since birth (Drenth, n.d.).

Unhealthy and Healthy

One of the biggest things you may have noticed about the Enneagram is each of the nine personalities has levels of integration, which range from healthy to unhealthy. These levels, according to the Enneagram, will continue to develop in your personality throughout your various life experiences. The Myers-Briggs test also focuses on the unhealthy and healthy psychological levels. However, the Myers-Briggs test states that you can possess a dominant level and an inferior level. While both of these levels are conscious in your personality, you don't notice your inferior level as well as your dominant level (Drenth, n.d.).

Conclusion

By now, you should be able to explain the Enneagram theory to anyone. You not only know the basic personality points, but you also know what their healthy, average, and unhealthy levels are. On top of this, you can identify their wing points, how they form relationships with other personalities, their subtypes, and their center type. With all these pieces, you cannot only identify what personality type you have but also help other people take the test and explain their personality types.

There is a lot of other information out there about the Enneagram theory. This book was a comprehensive look at the theory, however, you can learn more about yourself and others through further research on the Internet or through other books. Like many of the personalities have shown, people enjoy learning as much as they can about a topic they are interested in.

From this book, you should not only be able to take the test yourself and identify which personality you have, but also which level of integration you are on and what types of relationships you're capable of forming. It is important to do what you can to become the best person you can be, especially when you understand your personality better.

Bibliography

1 - The Reformer. (2019). Retrieved from https://enneagramawakeningschool.com/2019/01/09/type-1/.

Berkers, E. Introduction to the Enneagram. Retrieved from https://www.eclecticenergies.com/enneagram/introduction.

Cloete, D. Wings, Arrow Lines, Integration and Self-Mastery. Retrieved from https://www.integrative9.com/enneagram/wings-lines-integration/.

Cloete, D. 27 Subtypes, Instincts of Claudio Naranjo. Retrieved from https://www.integrative9.com/enneagram/27-subtypes/.

Dodge, A. Personality Tools: Understanding the Enneagram (from a Myers-Briggs expert) — Personality Type and Personal Growth | Personality Hacker. Retrieved from https://personalityhacker.com/understanding-the-enneagram/.

Drenth, A. Enneagram vs. Myers-Briggs / MBTI: Key Differences. Retrieved from https://personalityjunkie.com/12/myers-briggs-mbti-vs-enneagram/.

Enneagram Types. Retrieved from https://www.enneagramworldwide.com/tour-the-nine-types/.

Enneagram Centres. Retrieved from http://www.fitzel.ca/enneagram/triads.html.

How The System Works. (2017). Retrieved from https://www.enneagraminstitute.com/how-the-enneagram-system-works.

Hussey, R. (2017). How to Use the Enneagram of Personality for Personal Growth. Retrieved from http://www.artofwellbeing.com/2017/11/01/enneagramofpersonality/.

O'Hanrahan, P. Instinctual Subtypes. Retrieved from https://theenneagramatwork.com/instinctual-subtypes.

Relationships (Type Combinations). (2017). Retrieved from https://www.enneagraminstitute.com/the-enneagram-type-combinations.

Three Centres of Intelligence. Retrieved from https://www.theenneagramsingapore.com/three-centres-of-intelligence/.

Type 1 Subtypes. Retrieved from https://www.personalitycafe.com/type-1-forum-reformer/6097-type-1-subtypes.html.

Type Eight. Retrieved from https://www.enneagraminstitute.com/type-8.

Type Five. Retrieved from https://www.enneagraminstitute.com/type-5.

Type Four. Retrieved from https://www.enneagraminstitute.com/type-4.

Type Nine. Retrieved from https://www.enneagraminstitute.com/type-9.

Type Seven. Retrieved from https://www.enneagraminstitute.com/type-7.

Type Six. Retrieved from https://www.enneagraminstitute.com/type-6.

Type Three. Retrieved from https://www.enneagraminstitute.com/type-3.

Type One. Retrieved from https://www.enneagraminstitute.com/type-1.

Printed in Great Britain
by Amazon